ISBN 978-1-332-16060-0
PIBN 10292819

This book is a reproduction of an important historical work. Forgotten Books uses
state-of-the-art technology to digitally reconstruct the work, preserving the original format
whilst repairing imperfections present in the aged copy. In rare cases, an imperfection in
the original, such as a blemish or missing page, may be replicated in our edition. We do,
however, repair the vast majority of imperfections successfully; any imperfections that
remain are intentionally left to preserve the state of such historical works.

1 MONTH OF
FREE
READING

at

www.ForgottenBooks.com

By purchasing this book you are eligible for one month membership to ForgottenBooks.com, giving you unlimited access to our entire collection of over 700,000 titles via our web site and mobile apps.

To claim your free month visit:
www.forgottenbooks.com/free292819

English
Français
Deutsche
Italiano
Español
Português

www.forgottenbooks.com

Mythology Photography **Fiction**
Fishing Christianity **Art** Cooking
Essays Buddhism Freemasonry
Medicine **Biology** Music **Ancient
Egypt** Evolution Carpentry Physics
Dance Geology **Mathematics** Fitness
Shakespeare **Folklore** Yoga Marketing
Confidence Immortality Biographies
Poetry **Psychology** Witchcraft
Electronics Chemistry History **Law**
Accounting **Philosophy** Anthropology
Alchemy Drama Quantum Mechanics
Atheism Sexual Health **Ancient History**
Entrepreneurship Languages Sport
Paleontology Needlework Islam
Metaphysics Investment Archaeology
Parenting Statistics Criminology
Motivational

Mystical Musings

BY

FRANK L. DECKER

AUTHOR OF "POEMS OF PASTIME"
AND OTHER
MISCELLANEOUS WRITINGS

LOS ANGELES, CAL
1922

CONTENTS

CONTENTS—Continued

CONTENTS—Continued

THIS little book is not published to sell (if it were i would probably be a failure), but merely as a gratu ity with the hope of prolonging the *memory* of friendshi after that friendship itself has ceased to be. Simplicit and sincerity has been its paramount point.

Acknowledgment of it is not even necessary, unless i affords the recipient personal pleasure in doing so.

May its truth and philosophy console and comfor you when I lie, at last, in "the dreamless sleep that lull the dead."

F. L. D.

PREFACE

'Sometimes, when your heart is heavy and sad,
Sometimes, when your mind is joyful and glad,
Will you not peruse these rambling verses
With a thought of them that kindly nurses?

If I that way may be compensated,
I'll feel that we're in a way related;
And hope you'll follow the thought that's given
Unto the object from which 'tis riven.

May these mental pictures I have painted,
Remain on your mind, always high rated;
Through touches of joy and touches of tears,
Throughout the coming and going of years.

If there *is* a thought within these verses
That gives you pleasure instead of curses;
Let me to you, my adorable friend,
That worthy thought most cheerfully commend.

BEGIN THE DAY RIGHT

Begin the day right by doing first
The better things instead of the worst;
Then to the best of willing intents,
Control your temper at all events.

If during the day there comes worry,
Take things easy and never hurry;
When rising storms their fury expand,
Dispel them with a defying hand.

He who keeps from trouble and care
Defeats the end of many a snare,
And will feel with the coming of night
Acts of the day were rendered right.

Ethical rules are the best of tools,
And if taught in the rudiment schools,
Will fit us for those turbulent forms
We see in the skies when fraught with storms.

Time and talent is often wasted
Upon the things we've merely tasted,
And when we know their value to us,
Conclude we have been a blunderbuss.

Chasing the wings of so-call'd pleasure
Reveals to us an empty treasure,
And leaves its shadow upon our path
When we have felt the poignance of wrath.

Begin the day right and keep it up,
Will give us courage, and fill our cup
With the essence of joy, in knowing
There's pleasure in pleasure bestowing.

Begin the day right—God gives us might,
Good deeds to do from morning 'till night;—
And be it known when the day is done
A reward of merit has been **won.**

October, 1921

———————

—Four of the grandest conditions of life are: perfect health, clear conscience, contentment and absolute confidence in the welfare of our future.

THE CLOSE OF A PERFECT DAY

After the close of a perfect day,
    And night upon us serenely starts,
We feel there's something we want to say
    To express the joy within our hearts.

For at the close of a perfect day
    There ensues a peaceful, pleasant spell
In which our thanks we wish to convey
    To Him who thus has planned so well.

If we can recall some good deed done,
    Within the day as it is closing,
We feel a reward has been well won
    In which our minds are now reposing.

Flowers of the field bespeak at night
    That solace of the soothing sunbeams
We find in time of serene delight
    When a perfect day around us gleams.

There is for us some lesson to learn
    In ev'ry hour of a perfect day,
If in its beauty we can discern
    The constant glory of God's wise way.

Proud may we be of what has been done,
    Even in our meek and lowly way;
If only that good which was begun
    Completes "The *Close* of a Perfect Day."

HARVEST ON THE HILLS

(Between Santa Barbara and San Luis Obispo)

Golden are the hills that, rising high
    Above the sandy shore of the sea,
Outlined against a bright blue sky,
    Are exceedingly enchanting to me.

As waves the ocean, so waves the grain
    Upon the beautiful rolling hills;—
While during the months there is no rain,
    Old *N*ature here her function fulfills.

From early seed-time and the sowing,
    These hills assume an emerald hue;—
Throughout this season, they are glowing
    With refreshment of the morning dew.

But nothing remains long in one stage,—
    As develop the trees from planting,
So does our youth pass into old age,
    While we grasp at things most enchanting.

Where grows the grain from slanting hillsides,
    There is little change from day to day;
But, finally, as time swiftly glides,
    That vivid green has passed away.

Then in that stage of golden yellow,
    Between the blue skies and the blue seas,
The winds are blowing soft and mellow
    Against the ancient live-oak trees.

Wonderful sight it is to behold
    These lofty acres of waving wheat,
Since they have turned to gilded gold
    Where heaven and earth appear to meet.

Utility of this abrupt soil
    At first would seem an ominous dream,
But men in their determined toil
    Accept not things as they sometimes seem.

Man disdains the spirit of despair,
    While with glamourous hope his heart thrills
With the precious prize that he has there,
    In reaping the "Harvest on the Hills."

July, 1920

———

—Human life, allegorically speaking, is similar to a river flowing through mountain sides and tufted plains to the distant shore, and is obscured in the unfathomable depths of the ocean, never again to regain its individuality.

THE LITTLE THINGS OF LIFE

As sand seeps through the smallest places
    And slowly covers the scars of time,
So do our deeds of little graces,
    As up the ladder of life we climb.

Looking forward to big things beyond
    From trivial affairs of today,
We expect Providence will respond
    To numerous wants for which we pray.

As cement unites the granite wall
    And makes that wall a mighty power,
So the little grains that 'round us fall
    Produce the wheat that precedes the flour.

He who comes home with some little thing
    To eager children waiting for him,
Unto their hearts, happy thoughts will bring
    When time has pass'd and mem'ry grown dim.

A word, sometimes sharper than the sword,
    Leaves its cutting impress on one's heart,
And, if not soothed by love's accord,
    Forever remains a stinging smart.

The little things of life, knit like lace
    Into our every weal or woe,
Contribute to and fulfill their place
    As along the lane of life we go.

What seems a difficult task today
 Is perhaps banished by tomorrow,
And passed into the merest play,
 If all trouble we cease to borrow.

Smaller the bee, the keener the sting;
 Calmer the stream, the deeper it flows;
Clearer the bell, the sweeter its ring;
 Purer the love, the fonder it grows.

Incidents of life still linger on
 In constant thoughts of joy and pleasure,
And when the substance itself is gone,
 Memory remains a happy treasure.

Things that are small and trifling today,
 May magnify with coming of age,
As rare jewels in the matrix lay
 Prior to their most beautiful stage.

The little things of life, enhanced
 By affections that around them cling,
Remain with us in years advanced,
 And to our hearts fond mem'ries bring.

As flowers enrich the mountain side
 And sparkling whitecaps the ocean's crest,
So are the little things applied
 In a mystic way that serves us best.

October, 1919

MIDNIGHT MUSING

Caroline, oh, Caroline! can it be,
    As the midnight stars above me shine,
Thy beautiful face I ne'er shall see,
    Where oft we met by the ivy vine?

Dewdrops bathe the night blooming flowers
    That emit their fragrance pure and sweet,
As moonbeams light the enchanting bow'rs
    Under which we long'd so much to meet.

Autumn breeze, that with the branches play,
    Consecrate this sacred spot to me,
Where, the flowers fading away,
    I am thinking and thinking of thee.

The nightingale's song, that charm'd my soul
    Under light of the beautiful stars,
Has long since ceas'd, as the seasons roll,
    And leaves no equal to what it mars.

Birds that sang in the twilight of night,
    And thrilled the air with mirthful tune,
Have raised their broods and taken flight
    During the rapturous month of June.

Flowers that perfume the midnight air
    Have not the charm they once had for me,
When I was young with Caroline fair,
    And bask'd beneath the juniper tree.

Oh! can it be she has gone from me
    In the fleeting, futile years of life,—
Her face and form shall I no more see
    In this sojourn of sorrow and strife?

Then adieu to the bright shining stars,
    And adieu to the mild, mellow moon,
For they reopen the smarting scars
    Of felicity, follow'd by gloom.

November 27, 1919

———————

—As the proper frame enhances the picture, so do proper words enhance the thought that they convey.

RAVAGES OF RAIN

Down flows the debris of nearby hills,
　　As rivers rise from excessive rain,
Pitching, plunging with violent thrills,
　　As volumes of force they quickly gain.

Here a limb, there the trunk of a tree
　　Washed from the shores of raging stream,
And drifting away toward the sea
　　Like the rush of a runaway team.

Torrents of water from mountain side
　　Dash down with force of an avalanche,
As daring cowboys, for cattle ride,
　　When wind and rain is raiding their ranch.

Dark, dismal clouds hanging in the skies,
　　Foretell the danger of their fury,
As we take note that under them lies
　　The dreaded vengeance of a jury.

Then, with a rumbling of thunder sound,
　　And vivid flash of electric light
That wreaks the heavens and jars the ground,
　　The river pursues its angry flight.

Maize and grain that waved in splendor
　　With the western wind's gentle blowing,
From their moorings they now surrender,
　　And join the stream with fragments flowing.

Emerald valleys, coated with grass,
  Have been converted into lagoons,
As volumes of rain over them pass,
  And leave them in a state of maroons.

Devastated fields portray the scene
  Of this once beaming, beautiful land,
And the vales that were clothed in green,
  Alas, are nothing but sheets of sand!

But nature, like the spirit of man,
  Will rise and recuperate again,
As only forces of nature can,
  After the dire "Ravages of Rain."

February, 1920

———

—In looking over cards today as one often will, I find
names that bring fond memories around me still.

FLOWERS OF THE DESERT

Flowers in the balmy month of March
    Decorate the desert a brief spell,
Then increasing heat their petals parch
    As the sun begins to toll their knell.

Pink and purple and white and yellow,
    By myriads are blooming today
In an air of sweetness, and mellow
    With golden sunbeams that on them play.

Tender and timid, they now adorn
    The exhaustless waste of desert land
Where trav'lers, desolate and forlorn,
    Pursue their journey across the sand.

Bright and beautiful the blossoms are
    Against the towering, barren hills
That soar their heights in the skies afar
    As the vale with glory quickly fills.

Frail little blossoms of pink and gold
    Cover the ground with beauty and grace,
Presenting a scene both new and old
    Within the realms of this arid place.

Thrilling the senses with their daring
    And audacious attempt to survive
On such soil, the desert is sharing
    In its effort to keep them alive.

But these timorous little flowers
Growing under a balmy blue sky,
Not nourished by frequent showers,
Are destined to wither and die.

March 15, 1920

SONG OF THE CEMETERY

Sweet was the song of this fair maiden
That beautiful Memorial Day,
When with her voice the air was laden
On Sunday, the thirtieth of May.

Oh, could the dead have heard what she said
*I*n honor of their gallant manner,
When, with mortal wounds, they fell and bled
Beneath the furls of flag and banner!

But they hear not her song nor prayer,
That is borne away this afternoon,
Upon the mild, melodious air
That plays about their silent tomb.

Sad silence pervades the atmosphere,
As stare meets stare in a solemn thought
Of those who today are lying here,
After giving their lives for which they fought.

What could be more beautiful to me
Than that sacred song of Esther Dale
As I think of her over the sea
And think of her as "Queen of the Vale?"

WHEN I WAS A MILLIONAIRE

When I was a joyous millionaire—
　　Not in money as money implies,
But in youth; free from every care,
　　That later along life's highway lies.

It was *not* gold nor gems, rich and rare,
　　Bestowed upon my youthful years,
That made me more than a millionaire,
　　And leaves me now in the wake of tears.

But far more precious than golden wealth
　　The unbroken chain of kindred ties,
Endowed with happiness and health,
　　Before one of the family dies.

Father, mother, sister and brother,
　　*I*n the realms of home were with me there;
Then as a wife there came another,
　　Which rendered me a millionaire.

The golden treasure miners love best,
　　Lies hidden, with no way to show it;
So it is when we are in that zest
　　Of rarest riches—and don't know it.

Then fields were green and flowers ablaze
　　With the glory of life in their stare,
Proclaiming aloud with nature's praise
　　The happy sense of a millionaire.

But once the chain of joy is broken,
    We ne'er again can repair that loss;
And when a word of love is spoken,
    It helps us some dark river to cross.

Then to the youth whose future bids fair
    As over "the golden age" he treads,
May be reckoned a millionaire,
    As life's great landscape before him spreads.

But when loved ones have pass'd across
    The border land, and left us in grief;
We realize the depths of our loss
    As the midnight levy of a thief.

Thus it was, I beheld those treasures,
    That keep us from the sting of despair,
And embraced their passing pleasures
    In days "When I was a Millionaire."

May, 1920

—Some people are hard to analyze and hard to handle'
but the clouds generally indicate which way the wind
blows.

TIME'S TOLL

With another turn of Time's great wheel,
    And farewell to the departing year,
Effects of age we begin to feel,
    As the leaves are turning brown and sear.

We now demur on that border land
    Where brooklets turn to their final course,
And ramble away, as they expand
    Into vibrant fullness of their force.

How like unto a river life seems,—
    Bounded by landscapes on either side,
Leaving the past in the wake of dreams
    While pressing on to the ocean's tide.

Then often we think of years gone by
    In the buoyance and beauty of youth;
While now they're fraught with sigh after sigh,
    And remind us of that passing truth.

Like a beautiful river, flowing
    Forever toward the distant sea;
Could we maintain our youthful glowing,
    How sweet the journey of life would be!

Like a balmy breeze over the seas,
    Feasting upon supernal delight,
We covet the things our heart to please
    And darken our days by length of night.

But the meridian once passed,
    We start upon that receding plane
Which conveys us downward very fast,
    And fills our lives with sorrow and pain

There is no waste like the waste of time;
    Minute by minute the days pass on,
As onward, upward we strive to climb,
    Only to find our chances are gone.

It matters not much which way we glide
    On the sea of life, now homeward bound;
Drifting, drifting on the rolling tide
    Until at last our harbor is found.

Then like the ship from some far-off shore,
    Her voyage ended, and sails laid low,—
Ceasing our burden forever more,—
    We bid farewell to this fleeting show.

October, 1920

———

—The happiest hours of our lives are often but harbingers of sorrow that is to follow.

SOMEWHERE

There shines somewhere a beautiful star,—
 Somewhere in the celestial skies;
Across the seas in that land afar,
 We picture perpetual paradise.

Oh! beautiful star of wondrous light,
 Set like gems in thy heavenly crown
Above the darkness of coming night,
 As slowly the golden sun goes down.

Somewhere, there grows a beautiful rose,
 Beneath the shadows of myrtle vines,
Nearby the river that swiftly flows
 Through the rustic realms of pretty pines.

Oh! wonderful growth of forest trees,
 Where the woodman's ax has never been
To enthrall his soul with rhapsodies,
 And by cutting them, commit a sin.

Somewhere, there's a lady, beautiful
 As the flowers with dewdrops laden,
I'll frankly say (only dutiful),
 She's as "distant" as far-off Aden.

Somewhere, my spirit is reverting
 Through the remote rhythms of pleasures
  gone,
While she is deliberately deserting
 The golden chariot we rode upon.

November, 1920

IMPARTING TO A LETTER

Go thou little harbinger of peace
    From the roseate lands of the west,
Unto the faraway isles of Greece,
    Of which I am no longer blessed.

Convey to them my longing for home
    In this foreign land of adventure,
And tell them, too, I would rather roam
    Along the Aegean's low indenture.

Tell them of scenes wild and romantic,
    Far different from their native shores,
That lie beyond the broad Atlantic,
    Within America's open doors.

Take the tidings to those, who sleeping
    In the quietude of hill and dale,
To hasten from their languid keeping
    And for Hesperia quickly sail.

Farewell to your country and your friends,
    Farewell to scenes of juvenile years;
And look toward a land that pretends
    To replete the heart with joy and cheers.

Sever thou the bonds of home ties now,
    - And enter on those trying ordeals
That chill the heart and wrinkle the brow
    When one distressed and lonely feels.

Could we but find that heavenly spot
  So often pictured here on earth,
We might be happier with our lot
  In replacing gloom with joy and mirth.

But placing hopes on things forbidden,
  We find, when perchance they are attain'd,
They lie beneath false cov'ring hidden,
  And we at last have nothing gained.

Blessed be they who are *satisfied*
  With the resources at their command,
And accept them as first applied
  In the way they were wisely planned.

Then radiant was the Occident,
  For millions who have lived and died,
If, after the way their lives were spent,
  Could exclaim, "Lord, *I shall be satisfied.*"

November, 1920

———

—Parting of friends is like the afterglow of sunset, which prolongs fond memories of the day passing into darkness.

THE BLOOM OF BEAUTY
(*M. A. D.*)

I saw today a beautiful girl
    Whose hair was black as the raven's breast,
Her cheeks as smooth as the sheen of pearl
    And teeth white as Fujiyama's crest.

Her eyes were gray and mild and mellow,
    Her countenance as chaste as a child;
Her lips, the slightest tinge of yellow,
    As on her friends she sweetly smiled.

The precious jewels that round her shone
    Enhanced the beauty of her face,
As violets, after they have grown,
    Emulate the gold and gilded vase.

Sweet as the breath of flowers in June
    When fragrant fields are aflame with light;
Where bright sunbeams fill the skies at noon
    And moonbeams render their rays at night.

But sun nor moon nor brilliant stars
    In all their glory o'er land and sea,—
From Jupiter to the light of Mars;—
    Have no such beauty as Miss Marea.

The poppies have their crimson and gold,
    The lovely larkspurs their charms of blue;
But none the senses so firmly hold,
    As rosebuds bath'd in the morning dew.

Exquisite flowers display God's love
    *I*n the intricate beauty they bear,
And infinite stars that shine above,
    Convey to us His relative care.

Yet more lovable than the flower
    That retains within its calyx pure,
Resistance to seductive power;
    Is she who can temptation endure.

The bloom of beauty, often checked
    By the sinful folly of itself,
And its prospective pleasures wrecked
    By the act of a mischievous elf.

That perfect beauty we so admire
    Is the beauty we now seldom see;
'Tis the type that sets our heart on fire,—
    This matchless beauty of sweet Marea.

December, 1920

—Occupation is the foundation of happiness, and the idle are easy prey to the allurements of temptation.

CALLING OF THE CAMEO

Go thou cameo of mystery,
    Unto the realms of woman's attire,
And establish there a place for thee
    That esthetic critics will admire.

As to what may be your noble name,
    Origin, history and demise,
I have searched and searched in vain
    With the result of complete surprise.

Your face, familiar without a name,
    Has the brow of Clay and nose like Lee,
That brands you with American fame;
    But precisely *who* I cannot see.

Important, no doubt was your station
    As a statesman and a pioneer,
During early days of our nation
    When the future outlook was not clear.

If your presence aided those neighbors,
    In the ordeals they were passing through,
They prolong mem'ry of your labors
    By preserving this portrait of you.

This life is so short and uncertain,
    If we leave nothing our name to bear,
As soon as Time closes the curtain,
    Of us, others little know nor care.

It is the acts lying behind us
　　That are into the future riven,
And deeds of kindness that remind us
　　Of the blessings to us once given.

Then who wears this brooch in later years
　　Will confer honor upon her race,
′ And think of him whose picture appears
　　After others have taken his place.

December, 1920

———————

—If there is anything about us worth noticing, we will
be noticed.　If there is nothing, we will pass unnoticed.

CHRISTMAS IN CALIFORNIA
(*Dedicated to Mrs. Elizabeth Woolard*)

Lighted streets with wreaths of red and green
    Hanging in windows on either side,
And gorgeous garlands as ever seen,
    Foretell the coming of Christmas-tide.

Symbolic of our Redeemer's birth,
    We connect the sacred diadem,
With that eager state of joy and mirth,
    As it occurred in Bethlehem.

Within, there is a spirit of joy,
    In preparing this and marking that;—
To some a book and others a toy,
    If only a hood or baby's hat.

Both old and young are quite excited,—
    The parents in re-living the past,
The children now ultra-delighted,
    As gifts are coming and going fast.

Many perhaps are of little use
    Except to recall their childhood days,
When the wreaths are gone from long abuse,
    And naught but memory round them plays.

The streets and stores are one moving mass
    Looking for presents to please their friends,
Taking no time to talk as they pass,
    Where sparkling gems with the bright light
        blends.

But from the rush and crowded city,
    I long to be exiled and free;
For with the joy, there is much pity,
    And such surging has no charms for me.

Then through the long lane of pepper trees
    That leads toward the nearby mountains,
I trace the touch of a biting breeze
    That wafts its way o'er fields and fountains.

Beautiful is this fleur-de-lane,
    Sweet the clusters of pink pepper pods,
As o'er the road their branches entwain,
    And shelter the fading goldenrods.

At length, I see the emerald pines
    Standing in their glorious array,
While upon them the setting sun shines,
    Before the close of another day.

Then twilight falls on these lofty peaks
    That stand in silence 'tween day and night,
'Til the rising moon, in fullness speaks
    With all her force of impending light.

Oh! pretty pines, purified with snow,
    In majestic grandeur and delight,
That shadow the valleys far below,
    And crown the glory of Christmas night.

Los Angeles, California, December 25, 1920

LONELINESS

Oh! loneliness, intense loneliness,
    You cling to my spirit with despair,
And keep me in a state of distress
    That is heavy and hard to forbear.

The holidays passed in merriment,
    With much juvenile pleasure and glee,
For those, who through the excitement went,
    Preceding their merry Christmas tree.

But I find no more that youthful joy
    We so likewise felt in former years,
Borne by the spirit of valiant boy,
    But now, alas! never more appears.

As the trees, when their leaves are falling,
    Assume that demure, desolate spell,—
We feel the winter winds are calling
    To tell us of the season's farewell.

As calm follows the wild wind's blowing,
    And quiets the effect of its roar,
So is our mem'ry ever glowing
    With future hopes of life's open door.

Yet when we review the good and bad
    Under the light of their equal stress,
We are ofttimes sick and ofttimes sad,
    With the heavy weight of loneliness.

January 4, 1921

FLOWERS AND FRAILTY

(As seen in a Los Angeles street car)

She held fast a bouquet of jonquils,
    And acacia blossoms of the best,
Which vied with the golden daffodils
    That invited a floral conquest.

She prized these exquisite flowers,
    As the symbol of friendship and love,
Having brought them from ivy bowers
    That covered the arbors above.

She seemed to imbibe their beauty,
    As her countenance bespoke delight,
And lit up with that joyful duty
    The shining stars bestow upon night.

Her face, as sweet as the daffodils,
    Teemed in that beautiful array,
That the soul with effulgent joy fills,
    When rays of glory around it play.

To some poor friends in anguish lying,
    These flowers she kindly conveyed,
As if to relieve them, by trying
    Their sorrow and suff'ring to evade.

Who was she that clasped these flowers
    Within a hand withered and frail,
With snow-white hair, heeding *not* the hours
    That pointed to the end of her trail?

February, 1921

PARTING AT FOREIGN PORTS

With a look and a laugh and a sigh,
    As the ship's moorings begin to break
With waving of hands and sad goodby,
    Our final leave we prepare to take.

Friendships formed must now be broken,
    Perhaps to be renewed no more;
But mem'ry will remain a token
    Of the pleasant days at Singapore.

Farewell to the tropical flowers,
    'Midst many strange and primitive scenes,
Where we have passed some happy hours,
    And review them now as pleasant dreams.

The ricksha and little bullock cart,
    Ever faithful to their duty done,
Make it quite sad for us to depart
    Since our sincere friendship has been won.

Down on the busy, turbulent quay,
    Where all are hurrying to and fro,
The ship is ready to sail away,
    As the receding tides come and go.

And now she sails at exactly noon
    For the Malacca Straits and Penang
Then on to the city of Rangoon,
    Along the groves where cocoanuts hang.

Prolonged would be our pleasant stay
    In these equatorial regions,
If the great Malay peninsula
    Had not so many lurid legions.

Low, weird tunes those chanting natives sang,
    Beneath the shade of cocoanut trees,
That lined the streets of old Penang,
    As gently blew the Malayan breeze.

Then again we bid a kind farewell,
    To those we met in the torrid zones,
As the ship, under this magic spell,
    Sails away toward our distant homes.

BIRTHDAY BEATITUDE
(*Marea Dow*)

Stay, oh, stay the flight of passing time
    In that beautiful noonday of life,
Where I now stand on the border line
    Between the choice of maiden and wife.

Oh, must I leave the charms of my youth
    And enter the realms of womanhood,
To make myself in spirit and truth
    All that is grand and all that is good?

Happy days that came in younger years
    With the twenty-sixth of December,
Knew not the sadness of sighs nor tears,
    But only joys, as I remember.

The flower in fullness of its bloom
    Portrays the beauty of life today,
As I am free from that misty gloom,
    That, in the distance, will cloud my way.

Oh, could I stay the joy of this day
    And remain in its height of pleasure,
All days would be as the days of May,
    And make my life one golden treasure!

Buoyant ambition and buoyant strength
    Bless me now in the fullness of life;
But the days of joy, *shorter in length*,
    Will change into the cares of a wife.

Then as Time's wheel onward revolves,
    Changing today into tomorrow;
I pray the things that it involves,
    Be free from trouble and free from sorrow.

But like the radiance of flowers
    That reach perfection, then quickly fade,
We must bid farewell to youthful hours,
    And cast our lot with the evening shade.

Although the skies are sometimes brightest
    Just before the placid close of day;
Whereas the heart is likewise lightest,
    When the clouds of life have clear'd away.

December 26, 1919

VAGUENESS OF VISION

As rears the crown of some mountain peak
    Far away across the interim,
So do thoughts from you appear to speak
    From out beyond the horizon's rim.

THE BEAT*I*TUDE OF BEING

We plead to the earth and to the skies
    For something needed every day,
While echo rings with a voice that cries
    For help within us throughout the way.

The soil will open the planted seeds
    That lie within its viable source,
And light above will supply their needs
    As soon as they have taken their course.

We must therefore from the very start,
    Assist in that we wish to obtain,
By a constant effort on our part,
    And *earn* what we are trying to gain.

Our time and talent is often lost
    Upon the follies that round us play,
And when we stop to compute the cost,
    It leaves us in a state of dismay.

The earth and air have every where
    The requisites for eternal good,
And we can discern that they are there
    When nature by us is understood.

Energy spent correcting errors
    Is a loss to.us and loss to those
That fill our lives with mental terrors
    And shapes the tree as the sapling grows.

The ocean in all her majesty,
   The stars in their infinite array,
Have not the charms that thou hast for me
   At the dawn of morn and close of day.

The landscapes have those golden flowers
   That enhance their beauty day and night,
, And shed their sweetness in moonlit hours
   Upon the grand and glorious sight.

When flowers of the field fade away
   And denote their days are numbered,
We, too, perhaps have not long to stay
   Where once with them we sweetly slumber'd.

Then they with the elements perish,
   · And leave a sadness in their parting,
Just as the loss of those we cherish,
   While yet our hearts are keenly smarting.

Thus "The Beatitude of Being"
   Whether it is human or divine,
Lies largely in our sense of seeing
   The objects to which we most incline.

April 23, 1921

ABSENCE

Oh, Madaline, dearest Madaline,
 I think of thee from over the sea,
Through the fleeting years since I have seen
 Your face, so fair and sweet to me.

Beneath the shade of tropical trees,
 Where birds of plumage above you sing,
And perfume of flowers scent the breeze
 That around your presence sweetly cling.

Oh, could you waft a message of love
 Upon the soft southern winds tonight,
It would be as the bright stars above,
 And thrill my soul with ardent delight.

But far, far away where mild winds blow,
 Where every day is summer day,—
Where flowers bloom and pineapples grow,
 As natives chant on their homeward way.

I think of thee at the dawn of day,
 When the early light is pouring through
The eastern skies in gorgeous array,
 And drying the drops of morning dew.

I think of thee as the sun sinks low,
 And the shades of night begin to fall
Upon the scenes that around me flow
 Of other days that *I* now recall.

Far out over the blue Pacific,
    Where the stars so beautifully rise,
On the billows that roll terrific,
    Toward the Island of Paradise.

There, in that mystic land of flowers,
    I long to be with my Madaline
'And renew the old time happy hours
    By the crimson bouganvilia vine.

My presence there perhaps she will miss,
    As the surf rolls up against the shore,
And she looks into that deep abyss
    From the Pali's vast and open door.

Then, as she stands on that precipice,
    O'erlooking the tranquil vale below,
May it hold her in a spell of bliss,
    That only such sweet sensations know.

When the soul in rapturous delight,
    Has found the limit of its longing,
Like birds, in their gregarious flight,
    Other lands they want to be thronging.

Then will not my absent Madaline,
    From over the restless, rolling seas,
Return after this prolonged dream,
    And essay my heart once more to please?

February 19, 1920

RADIANT ROSES

Radiant roses blooming today
    In wondrous beauty we are seeing,
Perfume the breezes that round them play,
    And leave a fondness of their being.

Bees alight on their fragrant petals,
    And sip from them the sweetest pleasures,
While their crests shine like golden metals
    In these rich and radiant treasures.

Then fly away with the rose's breath
    Upon their soft, golden-gilded wings,
While the roses stand as still as death,
    And over them the oriole sings.

Beautiful, buoyant buds, bursting forth
    In all the glory of their rapture,
Caress the winds from the west and north,
    And delight in the joy they capture.

Bumblebees from the fields of the east
    Bearing golden-crested backs and wings
On these rich red roses, stop to feast
    And listen while the oriole sings.

Sublime depths of radiant roses
    In the glory of their grand array,
Where nature in her beauty poses
    During the beautiful month of May.

Garden City, Missouri, May 29, 1920

RAMBLING OF THE RIVER

Oh! glist'ning waters of merry stream,
    Rambling through arid lands of the West,
Sparkling in the morning's sunlight gleam,
    With vivacity, beauty and zest.

'From distant mountains, where storms blowing,
    Darken the heights of your lofty source,
While through barren lands, slowly flowing,
    You pursue a calm and peaceful course.

Dividing the level, crimson soil,
    Beautiful landscapes around you lay,
Where the Moquis roam and cowboys toil
    From dawn of morn to the close of day.

Sheep and cattle come over the hills,
    To take a draught from your shallow banks.
As their thirsty throats it quickly fills,
    And roundens out their sunken flanks.

Oh! beautiful scenes of western style,
    How bright the sun and blue the sky—
How sweet to linger here awhile
    Ere the golden day begins to die!

Serene the glimmering sheets of gray
    That stretch afar to the Moquis mounds,
As sunbeams on their hazy heights play
    And bask with warmth the surrounding grounds.

Then to the west, the land we love best,
 A silvery thread is winding on,
Where roams the Moquis with food in quest,
 Before the day is forever gone.

Antelope, perchance, may now be seen
 Emerging from the red, rolling land,
Where they will feed on the spots of green
 That appear between the drifting sand.

Onward, westward, serenely flowing
 Into distance and darkness of night,
Where sage bush and pinons are growing
 In their native glory and delight.

Western horizon changed to gray,
 Recalls that afterglow of the *N*ile,
Where so beautifully dies the day
 In the softness of its vesper smile.

The arena, now rugged and wild,
 As the river runs round bluffs and stone,—
While bright, white stars, their claims have filed
 Where the golden sun has lately shone.

Then through the gorge it forges its way,
 Under light of the beautiful moon,
Until at last, by the length of day,
 Its rambling course ends only too soon.

November, 1919

MEMORIAL

(Lines following news of the death of my old friend, William F. Bean, of Belfast, Maine)

My faithful friend of thirty years,
　　Now lies beneath the shade of trees,
While I meditate with burning tears,
，　　As mournfully blows the summer breeze.

End of the trail he reached at last,
　　After years of wand'ring far away,
From the early scenes of old Belfast,
　　But now, alas! has return'd to stay.

Dismal indeed is the gloom it cast
　　Upon his friends in different lands,
But deeper still the gloom of Belfast,
　　As she clasps no more his friendly hands.

A more noble man, a truer friend,
　　It has not been my fortune to know;
His life, simple and without pretend;
　　He formed that friendship sure to grow.

As flowers mature from planting seeds,
　　So man goes on from youth to old age;
Bestowing a record of good deeds,
　　Upon the constant throng of the stage.

But when all is said and all is done,
　　We realize the grave is our goal,
Unless another life has begun
　　With the silent parting of the soul.

Oh! then shifting winds of the seasons,
    Touch tenderly the boughs above him,
In deference to the fond reasons
    Of those who will forever love him.

It seems he is not dead, but resting
    Beneath the solemn walls of the ground,
Where birds in the green trees are nesting
    In their beauty and stillness profound.

Then may eternal peace surround him,
    While under the growing grass he lies:—
It is where the Creator found him
    And where He will command him to rise.

July 13, 1920

THE PAIN OF PARTING

Oh, the pain of this pensive parting
    As our sojourn now draws to a close;—
Like clouds on the horizon starting,
    Deeper and darker its colour grows.

Carlotto, Carlotto, is it true
    That our pleasures must come to an end,
As we now part in final adieu,
    After the time you have been my friend?

Then as the waves splash over the sea,
    And flash their sparkle upon the air,
Will you not think, think fondly of me,
    When I'm absent and you know not where?

The stars still shine and the waves roll on
    In the majesty of their being;—
And will no doubt after we are gone,
    When others their beauty are seeing.

Oh, could we prolong this peaceful spell
    Into the realms of eternal bliss,
How sweet would be the story to tell,
    Instead of the cold sadness of this!

But the weight of our painful parting
    Rests heavy on my conscience tonight,
And the sting to my heart is smarting
    With the strain of this sorrowful plight.

To us was given but a brief spell
    In which to arouse our fondest thought,
Then comes the hour of a sad farewell,
    And all is brought to an end and naught.

But those fond mem'ries will linger on,
    When looking o'er pages of the past,
And even though their brightness has gone,
    Their sweetness will still within us last.

September, 1921

———

—Fear and apprehension are two dark alleys that often lead to unnecessary and unwarranted worry.

THE MOON

Oh, moon, thou cold, white, radiant moon,
    That cast thy shadows in forests green,
Where balmy nights in beautiful June
    With all thy glory is now supreme.

Serenely, thou dost lighten the skies,
    And shine on my mother's grave tonight,
Where far away she quietly lies
    Beneath the shade of thy mellow light.

Mirrored upon lakes and rivers,
    Thy rays pour through the emerald trees,
And leaves the leaf that gently quivers
    In the sweetness of a summer breeze.

Like jewels in their nightly luster,
    Thy beauty pervades the earth below,
And myriads of stars round thee cluster
    *I*n infinite depths we cannot know.

The night, now calm with thy presence spread,
    Is more sublime than the light of day,
Reminding us of those that are dead
    And all but mem'ry passed away.

From Arabia's bleak and barren lands,
    To the sultry shores of Singapore,
Thy glorious light upon them stands,
    And enchants the scene forever more.

Beneath the shade of hemlock and pine,
  There flow little rushing, rambling streams,
That reflect the light almost divine,
  From under thy mild, nocturnal beams.

Then far away over land and sea,
  Thy light falls fast on the mammoth waves,
And renders there that tranquillity
  We find in looking on lost ones' graves.

Oh, thou beautiful, beautiful moon!
  In all the fullness of thy glory,
Thou fadest away only too soon,
  And thereby leave me sad and sorry.

June, 1921

THE FLAGS

We admire the great American flag
    With its colors of red, white and blue,
Though sometimes shattered like a rag,
    After fighting battles brave and true.

England, with her Union Jack flowing
    To the uttermost parts of the earth;
While France in tri-colors is glowing
    In triumphant form and native mirth.

Greece and Spain occupy little space
    In the realms of great nations today;
Defeated by battles taken place,
    Their prestige has long passed away.

And old Russia, ill led by the Reds,
    Has suffer'd the tortures of hell,
While her flag has been trampled to shreds,
    As beneath it her votaries fell.

Thus the flag has its triumphs and trials—
    As an emblem of justice it stands,—
Whether it waves in sorrow, or smiles
    At home or in far, foreign lands.

But the blue flags *I* behold today,
    Are *not* the flags our country obey,
They are the *wild* flags of *I*owa,
    That brighten fields in the month of May.

They live their lives and serve their calling
    That fills the purpose of God's wise will,
Without the strain upon them falling,
    We find in flags that have fought to kill.

Oh! then, hail the beautiful blue flags,
    As they grow along the green highway,
Where the wind upon them slowly lags
    During the rapturous month of May.

May, 1921

THE RISING SUN

Dawn of morning through the eastern skies
    Expands its light over hill and dale,
When first we view the golden sunrise
    That quickly pervades the silent vale.

Joyous songbirds emerge from the trees
    And charge the air with melodies fair,
While flowers supply the honey bees
    With exquisite sweetness hidden there.

Carmine streaks across the sky extends
    In brilliant and beautiful style,
While over the land its brightness blends
    And lightens the way from mile to mile.

I LOVE TO WATCH THE WATERFALLS

Oh! I love to watch the waterfalls
    And see their soft, surf-like ripples run
Down the smooth and slanting concrete walls
    Under the rays of a morning sun.

Onward, onward, forever they flow,
    In a mild and mellow tone of light,
As over them lifts a golden glow,
    And silv'ry shades at coming of night.

Then, under the charm of rising moon,
    There comes a spell of awe and delight,
That crowns the joy of twilight in June,
    For those who see this beautiful sight.

The quietude of night fast falling
    Upon these glorious waterfalls,
Reminds me of some spirit calling,
    As my captured heart it now enthralls.

Oh! peaceful falls of Saint Anthony,
    As wave after wave exhaust their force,
And die away in tranquillity
    While others follow upon their course.

How I love to watch these waterfalls
    In all the beauty of their raptures!
For within them, there's something that calls
    Unto me, as my heart it captures.

Oh, could our lives like Saint Anthony
    Flow on and on in joy forever,
How pleasant the chain of life would be,
    With never a chance for it to sever!

Yet as *I* watch this water flowing,
    I feel it ne'er will return again;—
Like human lives, it too is going
    To a final rest, there to remain.

Then farewell to these beautiful falls
    That charm this region every hour;—
Like stars above, their presence recalls
    *N*ature's proof of a higher power.

Minneapolis, June, 1921

———————

—The human tongue is often too subservient to the impulsiveness of the mind.

THE GEM THAT SHINES THE BRIGHTEST

The sparkling gem that shines the brightest
    Within my memory of the past,
Lies in the Alps, where not the slightest
    Cloud of discontent on me was cast.

Oh! beautiful spot that stirs my heart
    With emotions at thy sublime sight,
As raptures through me thou dost impart
    Where heaven and earth seem to unite.

Mammoth mountains in their lofty height,
    Rear their peaks to the ever blue skies,
Where we beheld to our heart's delight
    This dream of an earthly paradise.

Oh! then the grandeur of Lake Lucerne,
    That stretches away against the hills,
Starts the fire in my bosom to burn
    As my heart and soul it quickly thrills.

The silv'ry moon, with her subtle smile,
    Bathes the towns and trees in mellow light,
As our rapt'rous souls it did beguile
    In the charms of this beautiful night!

Fond dreams of these Elysian fields,
    As in their glory that night was seen,
Again and again upon me steals,
    As I saw them with my sweet Irene.

Brunnen, Switzerland, August, 1921

PART*I*NG

The vessel, now parting from her pier,
  Waves farewell·to those who 'round it stand
Are in the act of shedding a tear,
  E're taking leave of their friends at hand.

Adown the great river St. Lawrence,
  Where hills and valleys border her side,
Beautiful as the hills of Florence,
  The ship serenely and slowly glides.

Constant trees and towns and tall church spires
  Align this river along the way,
And tempt the heart with longing desires,
  Upon its banks forever to stay.

Then follows the tranquil spell of night,
  As the moon o'er the landscape appears,
And soothes the soul with quiet delight,
  That dispels at once all faults and fears.

But trees that grow and flowers that bloom
  Within the realms of their own abode,
Feel keen the sting of invading doom,
  When winter comes and their leaves corrode.

Oh! look where I will, the wide world o'er,
  I see not the face of Madaline;—
Her peaceful light shines on me no more
  But leaves me in the depths of a dream.

Faces fading in the land behind
 *I*mpress me now with deeper concern,
And the sharp sting of absence I find,
 Upon my bosom begins to burn.

But the ship sails out into the sea
 In all its vast, majestic being,
, While I am fondly thinking of thee,
 And trusting, trusting, without seeing.

Oh! could I but know that all is well
 . Beyond the sound of murmuring sea,
I would rejoice in this silent spell
 That now exists between thee and me.

Then let me implore the rolling waves,
 In all the glory of their power,
To serve us now with a might that saves,
 And keep us safe in every hour.

SHALL I MEET THEE *NO* MORE?

Shall I meet thee no more, Katharine,
    Must the parting of our ways come now?
Like the strange vanishing of a dream,
    I know not exactly why or how.

The fountain of friendship, vitiated
    Like grass that has famished for rain,
Has often been pleadingly stated
    In the wild wandering of my brain.

Time will not permit us to prolong
    Delusive hopes of happiness beyond,
As things by delay surely go wrong,
    And deprive us of that we are fond.

Years have multiplied, sweet Katharine,
    Since we were strangely brought together,
And at various times, it would seem,
    Our course has been through stormy weather.

In winter we look forward to spring,
    Then to the golden harvest of grain
The beautiful summer days will bring,
    And filling of granaries again.

We anticipate *future* chances
    And neglect the precious present,
As time upon us merely glances,
    And leaves but shadows of the pleasant.

Shall I meet thee no more, Katharine,
    As over woodland and plain I stray,
Where phlox and roses portray the scene
    In the beautiful gardens of May?

Where western winds sweep over the fields,
    And swerve the grain in ocean-like waves,
,As mighty warrior to warrior yields
    Before they go to heroic graves.

Then comes the dreaded "drifting apart,"
    Like travelers in far foreign lands,
That forever grieves the human heart,
    And leaves it restless as rolling sands.

Oh! shall we meet no more, Katharine,
    In the sweet shade of hills and hedges,
Where mid-summer cast its golden sheen,
    When first we form'd our sacred pledges?

Life's losing battles that we have fought
    Throughout the years of anxiety,
My soul with eagerness, they have fraught,
    And sometimes doubts of their propriety.

Then Kath'rine, must I meet thee no more,—
    Must I now forego this earthly bliss
Until, perchance, upon heaven's shore,
    We may abridge the present abyss?

March 1, 1920

THE RAIN

(Dedicated to my only sister, Alvaretta Decker)

Falling of the drizzling, northeast rain
    Upon low roofs of narrow sheeting,
Brings old memories to me again,
    Of years gone by and years now fleeting.

Out on the emerald, rolling hills,
    Fall a thousand drops for ev'ry grass,
And serenely run into the rills,
    That along their bound'ry quickly pass.

Rain, gentle, nourishing, needed rain
    That revives growing grass and flowers,
And refreshens the green fields of grain
    By mild and intermittent showers.

Steady falls the rain on hill and dale;
    The clouds are heavy and dense and dark;
While sheets of water lie in the vale,
    And submerge the nest of meadow lark.

My sister will know what this implies,
    When she looks over fields we crossed,
Where stood the water from leaky skies,
    And bewilder'd birds their nests had lost.

Trickling down the glossy window pane
    Rain drops leave their promiscuous trail
Like straws scatter'd by a hurricane,
    Or the prints of a prowling rat's tail.

Cloud after cloud sweeps over the hills,
　　Dispersing rain to the thirsty land,
Like wave of the sea when spray it spills
　　Upon the drifting and shifting sand.

Down drops the rain, in pattering sound,
　　Like distant rumbling of waterfalls,
That leap from heights to the level ground,
　　And flow away to the echo calls.

Oh, then spare not the glorious rain,
　　As it restores the fruit and flowers
Throughout the country of hill and plain
　　And semi-barren city bowers.

Little drops dash down the garden lane,
　　And are absorbed by atmosphere,
But fill the purpose of precious rain
　　Before they vanish and disappear.

Then welcome anew the gladsome rain,
　　As it prevails over land and sea;—
Its timely fall is our earthly gain,
　　Its pleasant sound, a solace to me.

ENROUTE TO ROME

From out the tunnels dark and gloomy,
    Hills and valleys of emerald hue,
Spread forth their vista, broad and roomy,
    Beneath the skies of a turquoise blue.

Snow-white oxen to the plowman's word,
    Hitched two and two and sometimes four,
Move slowly on and are scarcely heard,
    As they invert the soil more and more.

Festoons of grape-vines unite the trees,
    Over hill and dale forever more,
While gently blows a refreshing breeze,
    As the sunlight through their branches pour.

Tall towers of stone above them rise,
    In their loftiness, past and present,
Where, beneath the blue Italian skies,
    They picture scenes forever pleasant.

Further on, the turbulent Tiber
    Flows serenely t'ward the nearby sea,
Where wreaths of green and growing fiber
    Enhance the beauty still dear to me.

The pure white cattle with spreading horns
    Traverse the valleys at close of day,
Where blooming flowers are mix'd with thorns
    As the evening sunbeams round them play.

Thus dies the day of romantic scenes
    In the vesper spell of setting sun,
Where falls the glow of its after sheens
    Upon the night that has just begun.

Roma, Agosto 17, 1921

COME

Come with me where the oranges grow,
And the sun shines with a golden glow;—
Where the aster and rose ever vie
And the sweet daffodils never die.

Come where the palm trees wave to the breeze
As they waft their shade toward the seas;
Oh! come with your friend and take a chance
In this lovely land of sweet romance.

Come where the flowers are fresh and bright,
And calm days close to the charms of night;—
Where soft winds blow o'er the nearby shore,
And the waves roll on forever more.

Come with me where this beauty is seen,
Where the skies are blue and land is green;
For it is there my heart longs to be
In realms of joy forever with thee.

September 8, 1921

LINES TO A LADY ON HER BIRTHDAY

As rivers fed from fountain and spring,
May true happiness your Birthday bring;
One by one the years pass swiftly by
And test the friendship 'tween you and I.

I feel the loss of your presence now,
And to condone it, *I* know not how;
Yet if my loss is your secret gain,
From constant urging I must refrain.

Deeper the pangs of my wounded heart,
Deeper the sting of its poignant smart,
Under the strain I try to befriend
One whom *I* shall love to the end.

It is the love we see receding
That sets our hearts again to bleeding,
And knowing thus there is a reason
For what we call a bitter treason.

Could I command the touch of your hand,
And bind my brow with that sacred strand
We bestow on those we understand,
When that matures which we had planned.

But the fountain streams, like phantom dreams,
Wait not upon our belated means;
They vanish away ere close of day
And leave a debt of regret to pay.

Oh! could I impress the joyfulness,
If on your birthday I might caress
Those lovely lips, so sweet to me,
But now, alas! I seldom see.

December 26, 1920

MY VALENTINE

Oh, could I send this fond thought of mine
    Over the long and selected wires,
I would proclaim you my valentine,
    With all the force of my heart's desires.

A message of love *I* fain would start
    Upon the golden wings of pleasure,
Laden with the substance of my heart
    For you, yes, you, my precious treasure.

Then let me impart this thought to thee,
    As the moon and stars forever shine,
I'll freely submit my ardent plea,
    If thou will but be my valentine.

ALONG THE COUNTRY ROADS

Over hills and dales the motors run,
As on their journey they have begun;
By the clouds of dust they leave their trail
And meet the man who carries the mail.

Birds now singing in the hawthorn trees,
Fill the air with mirthful melodies,
While flowers, blooming beside the way,
Complete the charm of a perfect day.

Each bird and bee, I can plainly see,
Has for its shelter some waving tree,
But soar away to the fields around
To gather food from the fertile ground.

After feasting on the grain and grass,
They hum and sing to people that pass,
Then renew their flight in cheerful sound,
On their happy journey homeward bound.

Thorny hedges by the smooth, straight roads,
Shade the horses in drawing their loads,
As up hill and down they speed along
With a constant choice 'tween right and wrong.

Children now hurrying on to school,
Excite the brawl of the stupid mule,
And cattle in the fields are grazing,
With golden sun upon them blazing.

Emerald fields, that we now behold,
Will soon take on the color of gold,
And wave with the winds morning and noon,
Under the skies of beautiful June.

Retreating squirrels from bough to bough
Leap o'er the brooks that beneath them flow,
And the streams are fraught with frogs and toads,
As we glide "Along the Country Roads."

May, 1921

MEMOIR, TWENTY-FIFTH WEDDING ANNIVERSARY
(Mr. and Mrs. West, March 25, 1921)

Five and twenty years ago today,
These young folks set out upon their way
Across the plain of married life,
As it appeared with joy and strife.

Over hill and dale their journey wound
Through the trying paths of stony ground;
But youth and vigor buoyed them on
As sunshine comes after clouds have gone.

When trials and troubles upon them fell,
To one another they'd often tell
Of hope they had from heaven above,
Founded upon the purest of love.

There is no knowing what can be done
When two hearts unite and work as one;
Their strength, more than doubly multiplied
By standing firm at each other's side.

As a tree may rise or fall alone,
So with man and wife 'tis clearly shown
That if through storms they stick together,
There will be calm and clearer weather.

Happy are they who can steer their way
Through life's little squalls from day to day,
And then at night, when the stars are bright,
Repose in rest, feeling all is right.

Married life, like the struggling trees,
Embraces winter's cold, icy breeze;
And when they review their journey west
They think, perhaps, it was for the best.

There were at times some trying ordeals,
And thought of hardships still o'er us steals,
As we recall struggles of the past,
That upon our hearts their shadows cast.

It is consoling to you, Mr. West,
To know in trouble, you've stood the test,
And after these five and twenty years
Yourself and wife have no bitter tears.

May you remain in realms of flowers,
While traveling through life's mated hours,
And continue long this golden age
That now surrounds your happiest stage.

We are glad, in this way, to attest
Our kind regards for Mr. and Mrs. West,
And hope their future will long be fraught
With fond mem'ries of our present thought.

COMPANIONSHIP

Oh! come walk with me and talk with me,
    And watch the sparkling rivers run
From the golden valleys to the sea,
    That lies toward the setting sun.

Through forest and field they glide along
    Serenely as the heavens above;—
To youth and old age they sing a song
    That thrills the soul with heavenly love.

Like the birds and bees that dwell in trees,
    They acclaim their joy every hour,
And soothe our troubles as lotus leaves
    Soothe the waters with magic power.

The landscape of life before us lies,
    *I*f we but behold its beauty dawn
O'.er the gilded dome of sunlit skies,
    And claim our own e'er the years are gone.

Oh! then walk with me and talk with me,
    And sing the lyrics that cheer our way,
As mirthful birds in the hawthorn tree
    *C*heer the melodious month of May.

*C*ome, walk with me in that balmy street,
    Where orange blossoms perfume the air,—
Where men and maidens are want to meet,
    And feast upon the charms that are there.

Our pathway now is strewn with flowers,
    And beautiful views before us rise,
As serenely pass the golden hours
    That beckon us on to paradise.

Then let us walk and talk together,
    Along the channels that guide our way;
Though cloudy sometimes be the weather,
    Sunbeams will again around us play.

April, 1921

TO THE ENDS OF THE RAINBOW

While the summer days last, let us go,—
    You and I—to that enchanted land,
Where arches the beautiful rainbow
    Over golden hills and silvery strand.

Let us traverse that landscape and plain,
    Where fields and forests before us lay,
Until we reach the highlands of Maine,
    At the close of a sweet summer day.

Delicate colors of the rainbow
    Taint the skies in marvelous attire,
With the changing shades that come and go,
    From palest hue to the depths of fire.

Oh, let us fly in realms of the sky
    To the distant ends of the rainbow;
For 'tis there the golden treasures lie,
    And there where the purest waters flow.

After showers, the rainbow appears
    As a pledge that the storm has ceased,
And allays any apprehending fears
    By its presence in faraway east.

We think over there, there is no care
    To disturb the peaceful, pleasant soul;—
And 'tis there that all is bright and fair
    With the delusive rainbow our goal.

The roses proclaim their pink and red,
    The violets their velvet of blue,
But rainbows, their exquisite tints shed
    Upon the troubled skies they subdue.

Then let us fly through the balmy sky
    To ends of the romantic rainbow;
Where beneath its arch, rich treasures lie,
    For all we think and for all we know.

ANIMAL LIFE

(Assuming that man belongs to the Animal Kingdom)

As squirrels inhabit the highest trees
    And fish the depths of the lurid ocean,
So does man, in his mean extremities,
    Have ideals of a similar notion.

It depends upon the creature that lives
    In the woods or water or atmosphere,
Whether or not the environment gives
    Adequate pleasure for the time he's here.

But venturesome man explores dark regions
    In the remotest precincts of the earth
And there discovers the mystic legions
    That divert him to his primitive birth.

TICK OF THE TELEGRAPH

It makes the world weep and makes it laugh,
This constant tick of the telegraph;
From over the seas it brings the news,
Of kings and crowns and suffering Jews.

There comes a flash, Peru is shaken,
And many lives by earthquake taken;
Followed by some sad disaster,
Upon the shores of Madagascar.

Then comes the battle of bulls and bears
And the rise and fall of railroad shares,
With stocks and steel of various wealth,
Stating perchance, the President's health.

From under the sea the cables bring
The latest acts of Belgium's king,
And declares the trouble in Ireland
Is expanding with an iron hand.

Report of many crimes in New York
And more rioting direct from Cork;
Then the news of Bohemia's battle
With the famine of food and cattle.

Over distant plain and mountain peaks
The busy wire with sensation reeks,
Till the latest news from all the world
Throughout the country has been hurled.

Wonderful is the work they display
In conveying news from far away;—
*I*t barely transpires in Tokyo
Until by the wires we fully know.

Attracted by the familiar sound,
I like to linger upon the ground,
And mingle with the fraternal staff,
Where rings the tick of the telegraph.

But, oh, the speed of dots and dashes,
As through my mind there quickly flashes
Words of which *I* can catch only half,—
This rapid "Tick of the Telegraph."

January, 1921

TRIBUTARY OF THE TWEED

Down beneath the green and golden hills
    That enclose the little silver stream,
My soul it charms and my soul it thrills
    With sylvan touch of a perfect dream.

Thousands of sheep and a thousand hills
    Animate the view in living white,
While the stream flows on in murm'ring rills,
    Flashing its mirrors all day and night.

On its banks grow the Scottish blue bells,
    On the hillsides are hedges of green,
Where sky and earth in enchanting spells
    Vie and revel in this glorious scene.

Straight fences of stone divide the dells
    That bound this beautiful crystal thread,
And the bloom of flow'rs with sweetness smells,
    Where ancient warriors' wounds have bled.

But peaceful now is this tranquil vale,
    Where runs the river with rapid speed
Against the force of a gentle gale,
    And helps to swell the romantic Tweed.

Melrose, Scotland, July 22, 1921

THE PEPPER AND PO*IN*SETTIA

Said the pepper to the poinsettia:—
    "I am dressing in crimson and green,
To please my adoring Mayetta,
    As the most beautiful sight she's seen."

The poinsettia, in striking bright red,
    Replied with an air of sharp conquest:—
"Your colors are decidedly dead,
    And the world alone will judge the rest."

"Pretty pink pods in garlands galore,
    Half hidden beneath the shreds of green,
My beauty creates a great furore
    Among those who that beauty has seen."

To this said the poinsettia: "I hold
    That our richness shows every hour,
As compared with silver and gold;—
    You are the weed, *I* am the flower."

This hurt the pride of the pepper tree
    As one who feels the sting of defeat,
And in its efforts it tried to be
    *I*n every way, the most complete.

The poinsettia, in gorgeous array,
    Smiles merrily on the gardens green,
And in so making this grand display
    Pleases the heart of fair Madaline.

Then being brought to the final test
    (Between Mayetta and Madaline),
Both admit they know no bounds of zest,
    In the enchantments of this day dream.

November, 1921

———————————

—Inexperience is the key that locks the door of understanding.

FASCINATION OF THE FLOWERS

The exquisite charm of a flower
    As it expands in pristine purity,
Implies that the Creator's power
    Lies in its strength of security.

Beautiful flowers of perfect form,
    Soft as the evening shades of twilight;—
Yet holding their own through wind and storm,
    Presenting a grand and gorgeous sight.

First appears the early narcissus,
    In the golden depths of its beauty,
As the debonair, bashful misses
    Enters upon her maiden duty.

Then come the lily and peony
    In the rare richness of their glory,
To please alike, child and madonna,
    As they revive the Easter story.

Springtime with her copious flowers,
    Passes swiftly into summer days,
Leaving a mem'ry of happy hours
    That, deep within us, forever stays.

Larkspurs of radiant sapphire blue,
    Intermix'd with marigolds and phlox;
While asters, in their varied hue,
    Are blushing beneath the hollyhocks.

Oh, sweet blossoms of ultra-brightness,
    Beaming with beauty on vale and knoll;
Filling the heart with joyful lightness,
    While holding fast the rapturous soul.

Yet the "fascination of flowers,"
    In the long-loved gardens of home,
Ceases not with our juvenile hours,
    But follow us wherever we roam.

Marvelous spells of little bluebells,
    And prolific growth of goldenrod—
Combined,—the wealth of nature tells,
    And the infinite greatness of God.

March, 1920

PATIENCE PROSTRATED

Marea, oh, beautiful Marea,
    My spirit, lowly and crushed,
Is longing and longing for thee,
    Although its voice is sadly hush'd.

Your face and form before me still,
    Enthralls my soul with that desire
We ardently wish to fulfill,
    While yet our passions are on fire.

As the ship sails away to sea,
    Leaving behind tenderest ties,
My thoughts revert to sweet Marea
    And fill my heart with longing sighs.

Oh, could I prolong that pleasure
    She sometimes imparted to me,
What a grand and golden treasure
    Her loyal love to me would be!

But I can see she loves not me;
    And after years, I realize
It is the caprice of Marea
    My plaintive heart to tantalize.

Oh, could *I* turn to stars yet bright
    In the firmament of the skies,
And be freed from that dreaded night
    Her growing coldness signifies.

But nothing within my power
 *C*an alter her firm decision
For even the space of an hour
 Without a frown of derision.

Then free me from those dark ordeals
 You cast upon my pensive heart;
For sorrow o'er me surely steals
 When it becomes our time to part.

Oh, free me, free me, for all time,
 Of mental pain you cause me now;—
It is a caustic, cruel crime,
 To wreathe these thorns upon my brow.

But I'll bear the sting of your will
 Without a murmur or a cry;
And fond mem'ries. my heart to fill,
 Will remain between you and I.

MELODIES OF MORNING

Melodious morning breaks o'er the hills
　　As fade away the shadows of night,
And nature in her glory fulfills
　　All that is good and all that is right.

Little birds begin at six to sing
　　In the branches of cottonwood trees,
Where the air with their melodies ring
　　As borne away by the gentle breeze.

When all is quiet at dawn of day,
　　These little blackbirds begin their songs,
As if on waking, they want to say,
　　"Oh, Lord, forgive us our daily wrongs."

Thus do they announce the light of day,
　　As it falls over the hills and vales,
Then quiet their songs and fly away,
　　Where melodies of morning prevails.

Grass and flowers give proof at morning,
　　Of their infinite beauty and song,
As their vivid colors speak warning,
　　Their brightness will last all the day long.

Again the birds, the little blithe birds,
　　Whose slumbers of others they're scorning,
Are up themselves and after the curds,
　　In the mild melodies of morning.

October, 1921

WILLI*NG*N*E*SS

If only that which is required
 Be rendered to our fellow-man,
We lose the strongest point desired,
 And defeat the object of God's plan.

He who merely his duty has done,
 As daily duty is bestowed,
Has not the favor of friendship won,
 But only the payment he owed.

Compulsion as a feature in life
 Renders us a tyrannical slave,
And weights our lives with sardonic strife
 From earliest childhood to the grave.

But if by our chosen volition
 We anticipate the Master's will,
We thereby create a condition
 Forever desirous to fulfill.

If our aptitude is in the right,
 We find the burdens of life are less,
By doing goodness with all our might
 And helping others their lives to bless.

Young folks, like birds in bramble bushes,
 Have an eminent sense of delight,
And are upheld in worldly wishes
 By that impending, enchanting plight.

The dawning of liberty and love,
    Impels us to take lessons from those
Who, like the swift soaring of a dove,
    From humbleness to heights, have arose.

Springs that bubble up and flow away
    In ecstasy of joy and delight,
Find that boundaries around them lay
    In the course of their romantic flight.

But at last they reach the distant sea,
    And are lost in the depths of the deep,
As man goes on through eternity,
    And wakes no more from eternal sleep.

As a river that flows to the seas,
    This life is a source of usefulness,
If our fellow-men we strive to please,
    And prevail on them our love to press.

Labor is our best friend in disguise,
    When performed with a willing hand,
And provides us that exalted prize,
    We regard as triumphant and grand.

The sting of compulsion is cheated,
    By cheerful willingness to *exceed*,
That which is so often repeated,
    Within the avaricious man's greed.

Willingness assists muscle and mind
    To mount the arduous steps of toil,
As spiritual light aids the blind
    Through the darkness of life's endless coil.

Father Time is a stolid fellow,
  But has a strength of beauty in him
That comes with the leaves, red and yellow,
  When they light the forest, slightly dim.

He renders man bright and beautiful,
  As ancient wine sparkles anew—
If he accepts work as dutiful,
  And seasons it with willingness, too.

Then renew the old, olden story
  That necessity is a blessing;—
The hoary head a crown of glory,
  And luxury ofttimes distressing.

Fine flowers grow in remote places,
  And furnish there an air of sweetness,
Where nature, in those perfect graces,
  Bestows in silence her completeness.

Then glorify your work with pleasure,
  And combat compulsion with a smile,
Upon the happy wayside treasure
  You will secure in each passing mile.

When we are put to the test of it,
  In various ways of deep dismay,
We plan how to make the best of it,
  And bear its precious prize away.

Let us make our narrow boundaries
  A beautiful garden of Eden,
As strong irons from the foundries
  Make the beautiful homes of Sweden.

Compulsion glows with divine meaning,
　　And glory appears along the way,
When constant beauty of its gleaming
　　Surrounds our lives like radiant day.

Cheerful willingness lightens the load,
　　When in the wilderness we are lost,
And mitigates the long, lonesome road
　　That besets our way at heavy cost.

The spirit is greater than the deeds,
　　And blasts the way to final reward,
As flowers produc'd by planting seeds,
　　Demonstrate the beauty of our Lord.

Our tasks, like the mellow dawn of day,
　　When the morning lights of summer fall
In their glorious, radiant way,
　　Are lessened by His kindly call.

With a willingness that cheers the soul
　　'Gainst the hardships of daily labor,
And buoys us on to the happy goal
　　That wins the friendship of our neighbor.

What matters then which way the winds blow
　　If by *willingness* we pave the way,
As placid rivers serenely flow
　　Through heavenly hills from day to day?

e   a , 1920

NAUTICAL NIGHT

Far, far away o'er the dismal sea,
The restless waves are calling to me,
But what they declare I cannot tell
Unless it be their tempestuous spell.

Unto the clouds above them blending,
A constant chatter they are sending,
Until at last, they fail to quiet,
The turmoil of a regular riot.

The sun now lowering in the skies,
Leaves a trace in which the moon will rise,
And soon the stars will brighter be
For having shone on the glossy sea.

Then bursts the moon in all her splendor
Upon the scene in which to render
The glory of night, over the seas,
When tempered with the spicy breeze.

Majestic meeting of stars and sea
Upon the plane of tranquillity,
With the beauty of the moon so bright
To crown the glory of perfect night.

Deeper the solitude now goes on,
Ere the morning hours begin to dawn;
Then as the stars slowly fade away,
Enters the light of another day.

September, 1921

A LITTLE FADED ROSE

Deftly lies a little faded rose
    Within the Bible's secure embrace,
Where age and decay it sadly shows
    As time its beauty tends to efface.

Emerald leaves clasped 'round its edge,
    Denote they perished in that hour,
While clinging fast as a faithful pledge,
    Unto the slowly fading flower.

How long has laid this withered rose
    Within these silent and sacred leaves?
I venture to say that no one knows,
    As the thought perchance some heart it grieves.

Distant the hand that placed it there,
    Distant the garden in which it grew,
Yet remaining signs of tender care
    That gave it the sweetness of morning dew.

Symbolic of the short lives we live,
    This faded rose portrays our story,
When all we have we would gladly give
    To restore that lost and latent glory.

At last, like the little faded rose
    Whose brilliance and beauty is gone,
We realize as age on us grows,
    We are less fondly looked upon.

Such is the fate of the faded rose,
    Likewise the lesson of all mankind,
As onward, onward, time swiftly flows
    And leaves naught but shadows on our mind.

January, 1921

SEPARATION OF THE WATERS

(Arch erected by Canadian Pacific Railway where it crosses the great Continental Divide in British Columbia)

Lucid waters from the mountain side
    Flow under this arch with merry force,
Marking the Continental Divide
    Before taking their opposite course.

"United we stand, divided we fall,"
    Does *not* apply to this parting stream,
As it descends Hesperian wall,
    And descends arid lands to redeem.

Beneath this arch, man can stand astride
    Of the waters from the mountain's breast,
Before they, with reluctance divide,—
    Some flowing east and some flowing west.

Like two bright boys in life starting out,
    This rivulet parts, no more to meet,—
Each taking a far different route
    As they render their journey complete.

Gathering volume with ev'ry mile,
    Through gulch and gorge, it rages frantic;
Leaving here and there a farewell smile,
    On its way to the far Atlantic.

The current toward the Pacific,
    Is now rapidly forging its way
With fall and force ultra-terrific,
    As it increases from day to day.

Dashing down abrupt, narrow gorges
    With the fury of a madden'd beast,
This river its western way forges,
    While the other traverses the east.

Passing wild regions of the glazier
    Through rocks and cliffs and evergreen trees,
It contributes to the great Fraser
    That leads away to the distant seas.

Then utterly lost in the ocean,
    With its fathomless depths of the deep,
Far, far away in that mild motion,
    It is quietly rocked to sleep.

But its companion has found its way
    Through a land of different legions,
Where, with six months night and six months day,
    It lowly lies in Arctic regions.

And if at last, this levantine stream
    Reaches the old Atlantic Ocean
How, liken'd unto a mystic dream,
    Is that dream to a truthful notion?

Then the Atlantic and Pacific
    Have each a share of these waters sweet
Within their bosom, so prolific;—
    Separated, never more to meet.

April, 1920

VISTA OF THE VALLEY

(From the window of an eight-story building)
(Dedicated to R. G. L.)

Beautiful fields I behold today
    That lie beyond the city's border,
And extend away, far, far away,
    In their grand and glorious order.

Thousands of trees blend into the scene
    That with the grass softly harmonize;
Portraying the tints of richest green
    Against the blue and billowy skies.

Cattle are grazing in distant spots,
    Upon the grass that around them grows,
While horses are seen in smaller lots,
    Along the river that slowly flows.

Vast, oh, vast is this enchanting view
    That leads away to the far northwest,—
Where the landscape stretches through and through
    And nature dwells in realms of her best.

The sun emits a radiant smile,
    With all the glory of its power,
As if the valley it would beguile,
    In this serene and sumptuous hour.

A slight sheen over the vista creeps,
    As sunlight pierces the filmy skies,
And a dimness on the distance sleeps,
    As the day prepares for its demise.

Then from these hills and emerald plains
    And limitless lands, *I* ne'er would part;—
But quiet my thoughts in soothing strains
    That here blooms the flower of my heart.

Oh, could *I* prolong this charming sight
    That thrills my soul with rapturous tune;—
, But, alas! like the coming of night,
    It ends with the beautiful days of June.

H., June 4, 1920

THINKING OF THEE

I am thinking and thinking of thee,
　　As we travel through fields and flowers,
And wonder, too, if you think of me,
　　In silence of past and present hours.

The trying ordeal we're passing now—
　　Only a touch of what's to ensue—
Starts me to wondering how, oh, how,
　　I ever can live, live without you?

'Tis truly sad that life's sweetest spice
　　Is sometimes lent its severest jar,
By suff'ring sorely that sacrifice
　　We feel when "so near and yet so far."

But seeds now planted within our lives
　　May latent lie for some wise reason,
If only the test our love survives
　　Until there comes a proper season.

Oh, then will you wait, if not too long,
　　For the clouds o'er us to pass away,
And let us join in a hopeful song
　　That our joys will come, both night and **day**?

Genoa—Milan, Agosto 25, 1921

SOUND OF THE HORSE'S HOOF

The old time patter of horse's hoof
    Pervades the silence of evening air,
Recalling to us with ample proof
    Those long ago sounds are getting rare.

The auto, with its moving masses,
    Rushes along on high geared speed;
Waving to those it quickly passes,
    As they swiftly take their joyous lead.

But faithful old Dobbin trots along
    Over macadam and mushy mire;
Filling the air with triumphant song,
    While the auto, perchance, bursts a tire.

Fainter and fainter the sound we heard,
    In the subdued stillness of night,
Vanishes like the song of a bird,
    After the bird has taken its flight.

How true it is we openly know,
    There is no shelter without a roof,
And with passing time, all customs go;—
    Likewise, the "Sound of the Horse's Hoof."

Albuquerque, New Mexico, May, 1920

WHE*N* THE BR*I*DGE BREAKS DOW*N*

When the bridge breaks down that bears me o'er
    The strain of silence 'tween you and *I*,
There is nothing left for me, therefore,
    But acceptance with a solemn sigh.

In thinking of the past and present;
    We are prone to cherish days gone by,
And dwell upon the things most pleasant
    That beautified our terrestrial sky.

Then when the golden cord is broken,
    We feel the sting of remorseful pain
And would recall the words once spoken,
    *I*f our lives they could unite again.

Longing for one who never appears,
    Deludes the heart and saddens the soul,
Throughout the months and throughout the years,
    That allure us on without the goal.

But hope clings unto the human heart,
    When all but hope and prayer has gone,
While courage again it will impart,
    With another day's approaching dawn.

Oh, where *are* those rays of sunlight now
    That lit the lucid skies o'er my head?
They cease to descend upon my brow,
    And all their glory for me is dead!

The bridge that spans this lurid abyss
    Is breaking under the strain of years;—
Where once it held the cables of bliss,
    It now is parting from its piers.

The tide of travel is hard to turn
    After once its paths are firmly made,
And reflective thoughts within us burn
    As sunshine is obscured by shade.

Yet the current of hope onward goes
    As he who grasps the coveted crown,
Like a river that serenely flows
    Regardless of "When the Bridge Breaks Down."

October 30, 1920

WILL IT BE?

Will the Father with divine power
    Restore us as the acorn now dead,
Is restored, in that redeeming hour,
    Like the oak when its leaves have been shed?

If the acorn bursts its prison walls,
    And produces another oak tree,
Can we not think the Master that calls
    Will from the grave our tenement free?

Will he leave forlorn the soul of man,
    Made in image of immortal love,
And cast doubt upon his profound plan
    To unite us with heaven above?

If he stoops to revive the rosebud,
    Whose wither'd blossoms float on the breeze,
Will he not wash with his precious blood,
    And restore us as he wisely sees?

When summer ends and autumn frosts fall,
    Does he not give the sweet assurance
Of another springtime that will call
    Upon the spirit in endurance?

Will he withhold the promise of hope
    From the souls of men that crucial time,
When in the mist of darkness they grope
    Before restor'd by his help sublime?

If matter mute, is changed by the force
    Of nature into various forms
That never die, will he in like course,
    Not change us from the state of death's storms?

Will the spirit of man suffer exile,
    After dwelling in its house of clay,
Like a royal guest for a short while,
    Then vanish forever away?

If he gives fragrance to the flowers,
    And those exquisite songs to the birds,
Will he not give to this soul of ours
    All that is meant by his sacred words?

March, 1921

GO, THOU THOUGHT OF *MINE*

Go thou, my restless, wandering thought,
 To far-off isles in tropical seas,
Where perfume of flowers, nightly caught,
 Lay on the breath of the mellow breeze.

Go to the Andes' stupendous heights
 That rear their snowy peaks to the skies;
Where the condor makes his daily flights,
 And the sunlight on them softly lies.

Go thou to the mountains of the Moon,
 Then farther still to Victoria Falls;
Where at the hour of morning and noon,
 The Zambesi to the echo calls.

Go thou to *I*ndia's most southern shore,
 Where natives live in primitive style;
Then to the gardens of Singapore,
 Where fragrant flowers bloom all the while.

Go thou, my thought, to the Alps' high peaks,
 Where downward dash roaring waterfalls,
For 'tis their beauty my spirit seeks,
 And to their mem'ry my spirit calls.

Go thou, oh, my thought of restlessness,
 To Arabia's bleak and barren lands,
Where sunshine falls with that torrid stress
 Upon the glistening, scorching sands.

Go thou to Scotland's sweet Loch Lomond,
　　Where pink heather grows upon the hills,
And forms that picture we are so fond
　　As the heart with joy it then instills.

Go thou to Greenland's cold, icy shore,
　　Where the Esquimo is cloth'd in furs,
And lives in exile forever more,
　　While the drifting snow his vision blurs.

Go thou, oh, my restless, roaming thought,
　　To that magic isle away northwest,
Where days and nights with romance are fraught
　　By the presence of one *I* love best.

Go, oh, my pensive thought, where thou will,—
　　From Alaska's wild, romantic land
To India's far-away Tiger Hill,—
　　And behold the sunrise, ultra-grand.

Go, thou anxious thought, this wide world o'er,
　　In search of pleasures thou would secure,
But learn, alas! they will come no more,
　　Without the pain man has to endure.

October 1921

OVER THE RHINE

Oh! Geraldine, to my mind divine,
　　When free from trouble and free from care,
She blithely walked over the Rhine,
　　And left her image upon me there.

The broad white band on her glossy hat,
　　Proclaimed unto a look of youth,
Those juvenile charms there is in that
　　We so admire in beauty and truth.

Her step was quick and her pose erect,
　　As across the bridge she lightly tread;—
Gone,—gone to be sure,— I might expect,
　　As over the Rhine she quickly sped.

Away, away, and from me parteth,
　　As hair from a maid's bright eyes blown back
And, lo, a pain in my heart darteth,
　　As I watch'd her take that wayward track.

Her face and form now faded away
　　Like floating clouds in the summer sky;
Yet there was something seemed to say,
　　"She'll come back in the sweet bye and bye."

When time is passing only too fast,
　　There comes a mystic, enchanting spell,
And the things around us seem to cast
　　A weirdness we feel, but cannot tell.

I watched her there in vacant stare,
　　As others were coming to and fro;
But I neither knew nor did not care
　　From whence they came or where they would go

Onward, onward, flows the roguish Rhine,
　　Beneath the bridge on which I'm standing,—
Thinking only of sweet Geraldine,
　　Where she perhaps will soon be landing.

The sun now sinking low in the West,
　　Casts her shadow upon the river,
While little canoes, under the test,
　　Strain their oars with a nervous quiver.

Then above the water's rippling sound,
　　There appears the form of Geraldine,
As her face is turned homeward bound,
　　Crossing again the beautiful Rhine.

TRIBUTE TO A TREE

(Words of one and two syllables)

There stands an old tough and time-worn tree,
That affords shelter for bird and bee,
Against the flurry of rain and snow,
As the seasons swiftly come and go.

Sheep and cattle lie under its shade,
As teams are seen toiling up the grade,
And men view it as a resting place
Before they complete their toilsome race.

Other trees, like men, have pass'd away,
But this tough old tree has come to stay,
And while its branches are somewhat shorn,
*I*t endures the test of sleet and storm.

Its daily shade circles half around
The slanting sides of the rolling ground,
And extends its shadows far away,
With the setting sun at close of day.

A hungry coyote may call this way,
Casting about for his evening prey,
But the sheep are gone to their corral,
While the tree holds forth in silent spell.

The coyote now has lost his calling,
With light of stars about him falling,
And looking round in dismal defeat,
He thinks it wise himself to retreat.

When all is quiet in dead of night,
This tough old tree takes solemn delight
In standing there, monarch of the fields,
While good men sleep and the bad man steals.

Beneath its shade, where the children play,
Flowers have bloomed and pass'd away,
Since first I saw this hoary old tree
In the early days of eighty-three.

A fond refuge from the sun's warm rays,
During childhood's happy, playful days,
And a shelter still for those who see
The constant charms of this dear old tree.

Oh, could we retain, like this old tree,
Our youthful vigor, how sweet 'twould be;
And perish *not* with the fleeting years
That bring us naught but sorrow and tears.

September, 1920

RETROSPECT

Late autumn leaves turning brown and sear,
    Recall to mem'ry one far away,
Although in spirit, I feel she's near,
    Through the hours of night and hours of day.

From the depths of thought, there comes again
    Her fond image that around me dwells,
Like scent of roses, that still remain
    To enthrall me in reflective spells.

We sometimes feel the presence of friends,
    When they are not within our calling,
Just as the sunshine serenely sends
    A glow of light before its falling.

We often feel the spirit of those
    Who have long since left this earthly sphere,
Are with us yet, as the feeling grows
    That they to us are still very near.

Leaves that are dead and drifting away,
    After serving their summer season,
Have pass'd into a state of decay
    For some profound and unknown reason.

So with our friends that are here awhile
    Then drift on with the tide of events,
And deprive us of that welcome smile
    Their distance and absence now prevents.

Oh, how I long for those hours once more,
    When gardens were green and landscapes bright,
As they charm'd the vales along the shore
    And fill'd my heart with silent delight.

The billows roll on and on and on,
    The nightly stars appear as before;
But the charms of life from me are gone,
    Since her fond face I behold no more.

SADNESS OF SENILITY

Oh! have my former friends forgotten me
With the coming of adversity,
And left me in the sorrowful tears
That come to men in declining years?

When we have no more the charms of youth,
There dawns on us an establish'd truth
That we are then somewhat mismated
And soon become superannuated.

The young today are so engrossed
With fads and fashions at any cost,
That he who is becoming quite old,
Feels the world to him is growing cold.

Then, as roses with radiance gone,
He has but little to look upon,
When the evening shades around him fall
And bring with them their darkening pall.

WHERE THE SUN NEVER SETS

There is a place the sun never sets,
    *I*n the relative sense of my mind;
*N*or is there trace of any regrets
    For having known a place of this kind.

A perfect pearl in the pleasant past,
    Surrounded by hues of richest gold;
As the sunbeams their effulgence cast,
    Upon the memories they unfold.

The oasis of this far-off land
    That remains ever fresh in my mind,
Is beautiful, glorious and grand
    As a lover of nature can find.

As the placid river onward flows
    Through those picturesque vales to the sea,
So do I find, as time swiftly goes,
    These are the places most dear to me.

Lovely landscapes of the British Isles,
    Where sheep and cattle upon them graze,
As the summer sunshine on them smiles,
    And the balmy breeze around them plays.

Could there be a more beautiful spot
    Than in this land of historic scenes,
Where one I met will forget me not,
    And abide with me in future dreams?

It is there that the sun never sets
    Upon the embryo of happy hours,
Where the impression next to me gets
    As morning dewdrops are to flowers.

Oh! then may the sun forever shine
    Upon this beautiful land of dreams,
As my heart for it is prone to pine,
    And its fond memory on me gleams.

October, 1921

VISIONS OF VERDUN

Lurid are the visions of Verdun,
    As they appear before me today,
Where frightful battles were lost and won,
    And left their sad impress there to stay.

The morning sun lights up the fields,
    Where the sluggish rivers slowly run;
And trace of tragedy still reveals
    The horrible battles of Verdun.

Buildings and bridges of ancient form
    Are filled with holes and crumbling down,
Like fragments of trees after a storm,
    When alien elements on them frown.

Walls of granite, badly shattered
    By heavy missiles of shot and shell;
And people left, are sadly scatter'd,
    As their subverted homes plainly tell.

Hillsides, defaced by dungeons, dire,
    And shell holes over the ground are thick;
Between the windrows of rusty wire
    That render the heart severely sick.

In the dismal darkness of this fort
    Officers and men were concealed,
With food and water extremely short
    As subsequent events revealed.

At last, fifteen men, driven by thirst,
　　Their tortures no longer could survive,
Facing death, in a desperate burst,
　　But only three returned alive.

Oh, that vast and beautiful landscape,
　　Where the Germans stubbornly massed;—
What a frightful crime this land to rape
　　And on it death and destruction cast!

But war regards no laws of pity,
　　And this wondrous valley was not spar'd,
No more than was the nearby city,
　　In the awful loss it has shared.

Oh! that valley, beautiful valley,
　　Devastated by horrors of war;—
Can struggling man cause it to rally
　　In richness of beauty as before?

Tall painted crosses denote the graves
　　Where thousands are lying side by side,
And tell the story of those poor slaves,
　　As for their country they bravely died.

Oh, tell me why all this carnal feast
　　Was brought upon helpless men to bear;
And why do those wise men in the East,
　　Such terrible tragedies prepare?

Looking over the rolling plateau,
　　Now frightfully marred and forlorn,
I behold that vengeance war will do,
　　As homes are wrecked and hearts are torn.

O'er desolate "*N*o Man's Land" I look,
 Where the darkest days and nights were spent,
As the trembling earth from cannon shook,
 And heavens above in twain were rent.

Argonne Forest waves her weeping trees
 To mournful winds that over it play,
In mem'ry of men from o'er the seas,
 That beneath its shade forever lay.

With strength and valor that man displays
 *I*n bitter battles here lost and won,
The strongest that human thought conveys,
 Is this baleful vision of Verdun.

August, 1921

FADING OF THE FLOWERS

Oh, beautiful, beautiful flowers
 That animate the gardens in May;
Must you, with the swiftly passing hours,
 Forego that beauty and fade away?

Too sweet has been the spell of delight
 In which you follow'd the winter's chill
To take so soon your lamented flight
 And leave no others your place to fill.

For weeks and months they laden the breeze
 With a fragrance that charms our senses;
While from their petals they feed the bees
 Nectar from which honey condenses.

Vivid have been their colors of June,
 As Southern winds blew them to and fro,
Bearing away their sweetest perfume
 O'er hills and vales to mountains of snow.

Oh! could *I* waft a message of love
 On the breath of these flexible stems,
As to the fantastic clouds above
 They wave their beautiful diadems.

But naught can stay their vigorous bloom
 As effects of time will surely tell,
When the autumn days pronounce their doom
 And resound again their solemn knell.

The violets, already drooping,
　　Are first to show the passing season;—
Like man with age, who, lowly stooping,
　　Pauses again to catch his reason.

Then, finally, faded and forlorn,
　　They pass into a state of decay;—
Of their main beauty they have been shorn
　　And enter a sad stage of dismay.

But they will return with coming spring
　　And blossom supremely as before;
While man, alas, no seasons will bring
　　That vigor gone, to return no more.

April, 1920

ABSENT

From afar my spirit is calling
 To one whose features *I* long to see;
While she, perchance, like dead leaves falling,
 *I*s drifting, drifting, farther from me.

With the tidal winds and roaring waves
 That caress the shores of Amsterdam,
My mind reverts, and my heart now craves,
 For the one who knows not where *I* am.

If, in knowing this, she could possess
 The depth of thought it brings to me now,
I'd better forbear the loneliness
 That hovers around my anxious brow.

From over land nor over the sea
 As the days and nights pass quickly by,
*N*o word of love ever comes to me,
 As my fondest hopes begin to die.

Absence prolonged sickens the heart,
 And deprives it of that state of bliss
Unto each other we would impart,
 Instead of forbearing things amiss.

Day by day, she is weaned away,
 From the sacred covenant we had,
Until at last, I regret to say,
 My spirit is dejected and sad.

Lives, crowned with garlands of flowers,
    See not the shadow that lies beyond
The horizon of those golden hours,
    In which they were so supremely fond.

Then dark and ominous clouds arise,
    Where radiant were the skies above,
While time and absence our patience tries
    And tests the strength of a sacred love.

WHEN THE LAWNS ARE COVERED WITH LEAVES

When the lawns are covered with leaves
    Drifting and shifting upon the ground,
In retrospect, my spirit perceives—
    The Autumnal wind's familiar sound.

Summer, with plethoric foliage,
    Has bid adieu to the fleeting show,
While Autumn enters upon the stage
    With her crimson leaves and touch of snow.

The atmosphere is crisp with ozone,
    The skies are tinted in azure blue,
And the leaves have taken on that tone
    We feel when the end of life is due.

Bending grass blades now glisten with frost,
    As the spicy breeze plays through the trees,
And flowers, with their brilliance lost,
    Can no more nourish the honey bees.

Leaves, once green, have fallen to the ground
    And changed into a semi-red,
While the autumn winds, with mournful sound,
    Denote with sadness that they are dead.

And thus it is, for God's wise reasons;
    The leaves are changed after awhile,
And fade away with passing seasons,
    But come again with a springtime smile.

Sweet summer leaves and late autumn leaves—
     How they depict our laconic lives—
Flourishing first, then our heart deceives,
     When hope within us no longer thrives.

Like unto the beautiful flowers,
     Life is buoyant in early stages,
But soon declines with the passing hours,
     And leaves us sad in our old ages.

Like unto a beautiful maiden,
     New leaves adorn the tree with splendor,
As her bosom, with jewels laden,
     Prepares her debut best to render.

Then in this glorious youthful stage,
     The golden days of life are passed,
Before she enters upon the age
     That clouds and shadows her path at last.

Like the desolate trees, void of leaves
     When winter winds have stripped them bare,
Man deserted, to his master cleaves,
     And clings unto the Creator's care.

When whisp'ring winds are faintly heard,
     My pensive heart with emotion grieves,
And I am sad and deeply stirred,
     "When the lawns are covered with leaves."

October, 1920

CEYLON

Ceylon, Ceylon, beautiful Ceylon;
    As a child of India far away,
I think of thee, and days that are gone,
    While yet thy memories with me stay.

Where palm trees wave with the western breeze
    That comes from o'er the *I*ndian Ocean,
And vibrate the tall palmetto trees
    With subdued and silent motion.

Set like a pearl in translucent shell,
    Far from where flows the River Avon,
Cocoanut trees, in that dreamy spell
    Pervade the lovely land of Ceylon.

Against the shore the blue billows roll,
    And spend their force in foamy white spray,
That enchants the scene and charms the soul,
    As the golden sunbeams on them play.

Withal, the rolling, restless ocean,
    That extends from this enchanted isle,
With its forever ceaseless motion,
    And murmuring music all the while.

Ferns and flowers and spicewood growing
    Beneath the shade of tropical vines,
Where all the stars within our knowing
    Upon this island serenely shines.

From *Colombo's* stately lighthouse tower,
  There flashes signals both night and day,
To guide the vessels every hour,
  That in their course, have called this way.

Ferns in the forests, gems in the mines;
  Ceylon is the land of far-off dreams;
With romance there as the heart inclines,
  To explore its woods and winding streams.

Rubies, brighter than the stars portray,
  Sapphires blue as the ocean beyond,
And cat's-eyes with that beguiling ray
  To which temptations quickly respond.

Colpetty, from town a mile or more,
  There leads a broad, busy thoroughfare,
Where the grass is green along the shore,
  And we watch the waves while resting there.

Sublime the view t'ward the golden sun,
  Sinking beyond the glistening seas,
As the dying day is nearly done,
  And the rising moon creeps o'er the trees.

At last, adieu to the skies so blue,
  And ocean's constant murmuring song,—
And the sparkling stones so rich in hue,
  Unto all, *I* say so long, so long.

Colombo, October, 1913

WEAVING THE WEB OF LIFE

Little by little, life is woven
    Upon the fleeting current of time,—
Composed of what we have chosen
    From the bells that ring with constant chime.

Childhood's season of seed-time sowing,
    Is buoyant with hopes of life beyond,
As the golden sun, in its glowing,
    Opens the way where the heart is fond.

Then comes the age of work and struggle,
    That on us now begins to settle,
When years of worry and of trouble,
    Tests the endurance of our mettle.

And weaving now the figures that last
    Within the web of eternal joy,
We look to time that is passing fast,
    To keep us from the sting of annoy.

As down the throngs of a busy street,
    Mingled with the sound of cobblestones,
We may, perchance, some poor pauper meet
    That time has racked his aching bones.

In the crowded streets of Amsterdam,
    Where old and young, rushing to and fro,
With ev'rything—cart to caravan—
    Comprises this promiscuous show.

Over the low lands of Holland fair,
　　Where sheep and cattle fulfill their place,
Young men and women are working there,
　　With eager aptness of their race.

Upon the smooth and sandy seashore,*
　　Thousands are breathing the balmy breeze,
While thousands are coming, more and more,
　　To watch the waves of the rolling seas.

The trying ordeal of life prevails
　　When bidding goodby to friends so true,
As our ship of fate now outward sails
　　And we wave a last, final adieu.

Then let us weave the web of our life
　　In peaceful justice, caution and care,
As numerous troubles and its strife,
　　Try our strength of endurance to bear.

---

*Refers to Scheveningen, famous suburb of The Hague; Holland's most beautiful beach and popular seaside resort.

THE TRAIL WE TRAVEL

As man's mustache begins to grow gray,
　　And little furrows invade his face,
He sees in the mirror, day to day,
　　Those senile signs that are taking place.

He then reviews the landscape of life,
　　And stops to reflect upon the past,
Where he, perchance, met and won a wife
　　When sweet maidens their allurements cast.

This life is like a stream flowing on
　　From its fountain source to distant sea;
The present is ours, the past is gone;
　　The future, we know not what will be.

Water passing a specific mark,
　　Never returns to that place again,
But onward flows through daylight and dark,
　　In its constant course o'er field and plain.

Swiftly, surely, our days are devour'd
　　By the inscrutable hand of time,
And our pathway may be showered
　　With the light of good or curse of crime.

League by league, roving ships of the sea
　　Complete their journey from shore to shore;
Guided by a helm, their course is free
　　From rocky reefs of the water's floor.

Thus the helm of this human vessel
　　Steers our voyage toward rough or calm,
While to that port we closely nestle
　　That shelters us with heavenly balm.

The tide of life, turned in a day,
　　Like the changing of a river's bed,
Flows onward in that still, rhythmless way
　　We feel when youthful pleasures are dead.

When golden days of summer are past,
　　And clouds are gathering o'er our heads
With dismal shadows upon us cast,
　　We feel that darkness before us spreads.

There may be a light beyond this spell
　　From which we emerge into that realm
Of a future, bright; if all is well,
　　When a higher power holds our helm.

March 15, 1921

ALPHA AND OMEGA

Adown the days of the pleasant past,
    I trace the travels of sweet romance,
That charmed my soul and held me fast,
    To a lovely lady met by chance.

With passing winter and coming spring,
    The alpha of our friendship was laid,
As the vernal winds fresh flowers bring,
    And joyous birds their appearance made.

The sweet summer days paved our ways,
    O'er the beautiful landscape of green,
Which spread before us in sky-lit haze,
    And render'd our lives a constant dream.

Soon autumn came with its frosty spell,
    Whitening the fields of growing wheat;
Then the snows of winter softly fell
    And clothed them in a fleecy sheet.

But winter winds had no fear for me,
    Their biting blast, easy to forego,
If her fond face *I* could only see,
    Regardless of ice or rain or snow.

Time thus passing, we scarcely believe
    There is an end to present pleasure,
*N*or that the future our hearts will grieve
    *I*n their replete and meted measure.

Oh, how glorious would be the years,
    If we could maintain this state of joy,
And banish all the trouble and fears
    That fill our lives with foreign alloy!

Beautiful woman of splendid type,
    That young and aged alike admire,
As the luscious fruit when it is ripe,
    Fills our heart with an ardent desire.

But golden grain that ripens today,
    In the beauty of its completeness,
Stands for awhile, then withers away
    As time destroys its first-born sweetness.

How sweet to trace the journey of life
    Like a winding stream from distant source,
As man, in the pursuit of a wife,
    Surveys its route of romantic course.

When friendship's chain has ne'er been broken,
    And links are welded by true regard,
Beware of those words sometimes spoken
    That leave a sting and blow that is hard.

There comes a time when friendship is dead,
    And its wither'd leaves around us lie;
From me, alas! their beauty has fled
    Like fleeting clouds in a summer sky.

Then ceas'd to bloom that beautiful Rose,
    To me so constant these passing years;—
For what or why, the Lord only knows,
    Unless it be to bring back the tears.

That there are "as good fish in the sea"
    As have been caught with the hook or seine,
Contains no consolation for me,
    But proves our designs often in vain.

All things have their embryo and end;
    Alpha, perhaps, leads us to believe
Its viable love it will extend,
    But *Omega*, we find, will deceive.

Oh, why hast thou forsaken me now?
    As Jesus cried out near the ninth hour.
You have broken my heart and my vow
    By the fatal blow of your power.

February, 1921

IF WE COULD KNOW

If we could know where they are today,—
  Absent, ardent friends of former years,
Who since have wandered far away
  And left us in the shadow of tears.

If we could know what they are doing,
  As distance divides us day and night,
Perhaps we might in thus reviewing,
  Live o'er again those days of delight.

Absence sickens and distracts the heart,
  As we imagine some things go wrong,
While feeling a painful sting and smart
  Where once we felt a jubilant song.

If joys of the future we could know,
  They would enhance our present treasure,
In looking toward their golden glow,
  With brighter hopes of coming pleasure.

If we could know the troubles ahead,
  Our present would be filled with fear,
And would thereby the dark future dread
  Before death itself was very near.

If we could know the fragrant flower
  Would bloom again in coming of spring,
How pleasant would be each passing hour
  As constant joy to our hearts 'twould bring.

If we could know some worshipped one
    Was to us true through life's ragged edge,
We would consider the right deed done
    In holding fast their promised pledge.

If we could know where abides the soul
    Of those who have from us departed,
How supremely sweet would be the goal
    For which in youth we humbly started!

April, 1921

POIGNANCY OF PARTING

In parting from thee at this late hour
    The sacred ties that thou dost sever
Deprives me of the sweetest flower
    And leaves a scar that lasts forever.

Friendship of fidelity and truth,
    As has existed 'tween you and I
From the earliest years of our youth,
    Can only be severed with a sigh.

Without thee, like a mariner lost
    In the infinite realms of the sea;
I feel as he whose pleasures it cost
    And knows not where his refuge will be.

NOWHERE

*N*owhere do I see the golden sunbeams
    Of hope and happiness before me now;
But annoying trouble slowly convenes
    *I*ts shadows about my furrowed brow.

*N*owhere do *I* see those fragrant flowers
    That thrilled my soul with rapt'rous delight,—
Where once they brightened the morning hours
    And sweetened the air of summer night.

*N*owhere do I find those old-time pleasures
    Of youthful enjoyments, dear to my heart;—
They now are lost to the shrunken measures
    We feel when vigor begins to depart.

*N*owhere is the dog that ran out to play
    When I returned to the old homestead;
As from the threshold he met me half-way;
    But now, alas! I learn he, too, is dead.

*N*owhere do *I* see the knotty oak trees
    That defied the vicissitudes of time,
*N*or smell the perfume of the lilac breeze
    That wafted its way from a southern clime.

*N*owhere do *I* hear my Madaline dear;—
    Like the lilac blossoms, she's pass'd away;
Yet as echoes of music *ringing clear,*
    Her image is with me both night and day.

*N*owhere do *I* find those sacred treasures
    That with passing years *I* fondly cherish'd,
And now recall the fleeting pleasures
    After their being has long since perished.

November, 1920

THE FIRST WHITE FROST

With October, falls the first white frost
    Upon the fields of wheat and clover;
Leaves and flowers their color have lost
    As days of summer now are over.

Foliage that was a vivid green
    Takes on the hue of crimson and gold,
While landscapes change to a somber scene
    That is akin to the coming cold.

Waving corn blades, withered and brown,
    Are chaffing under the chilly air;
While nuts in the trees are tumbling down
    With winds of autumn that send them there.

Flowers once bright their lustre have lost
    To the change that has over them come;—
With the coming of the first white frost,
    Their pride and beauty is stricken dumb.

The nightingale now no longer sings,
    The sparrow has ceas'd his arrogance,
The robin lies low beneath his wings,
    But the snowbirds start their merry dance.

The rabbit, somewhat demure and shy,
    Leaves triangle tracks upon the ground,
While the squirrel, his winter supply
    Has laid up where it cannot be found.

Birds and beasts feel this autumnal change
    And adjust their plans for cold weather,
While men and women begin to arrange
    Their early winter's work together.

And thus it is, with the first white frost,
    All things take on a different cast,—
Flowers, their fragrance and tint have lost,
    With winter coming and summer past.

October, 1921

THE BLACK MAN'S BURDENS

(Poem of Pathos)

The black man has his burdens to bear,
His toilsome days, his troubles and care;
Anxious moments hang over his head
*I*n planning how his children be fed.

When first he comes from the Sunny South
Where used to living from hand to mouth,
He branches out on a broader gauge
As he enters on his newfound stage.

His burdens now begin to arise,
As he feels himself of undersize,
And by the time his plans are complete
He finds it hard to make both ends meet.

Then comes the freezing northwestern storm
Without much fuel to keep him warm,
And poverty stares him in the face,
So common to the colored race.

His chances now look dismal indeed
As he has no one to take the lead;
He then thinks of the old southern home
And longs once more that country to roam.

Where palm trees wave and the myrtle vines,
And the south wind blows and warm sun shines;
Where cotton grows high and cane grows tall,
He loves them yet and longs for them all.

Oh, for the dear days of his childhood,
When, through the fields and through the wildwood,
He watched his parents on their way,
Coming homeward at the close of day.

Crude little cabin it was at best,
But furnished them a place to rest,
As night came on and darkened the skies,
His youthful face was filled with sighs.

With the days and nights thus oppressed,
He has a longing to go northwest;
Then bids adieu to the old homestead
Where times were tough and tears had been shed.

Sad were the scenes of humble parting
When this poor boy prepar'd for starting,
His grief was keen and his heart was sore,
As he said farewell forever more.

The cotton and cane now left behind,
He dreams of fortune he is to find,—
As the golden light of morning shows,
A vague hope within him quickly grows.

Palmetto and pine he sees no more,
As in his juvenile days of yore;
But after years, a struggle indeed
His hungry children to clothe and feed.

As prospects appear somewhat brighter,
His task becomes a little lighter,
But problems of life still very grave,
And he seldom can much money save.

The black man's burdens, no matter where,
Are always heavy and hard to bear,
, For he never has an equal chance
The white man's energy to advance.

October, 1921

ENGLISH ENGINES

(*Dedicated to Mr. W. J. Black, Chicago, Ill.*)

With bolts and bars mostly concealed,
    The English engines at first look plain,
But strength and beauty is revealed
    When they proceed to handle the train.

There's no noisy bell to jar the ear,
    But short sounds of the whistle instead;
Making easier the words to hear
    When they are given to go ahead.

Plain and simple as they look to be,
    Without the rods and without the bell,
There is something there we cannot see
    That fulfills its purpose extra well.

Painted black or a very dark green,
    With a narrow strip of deep red dye
Around the margin, plain to be seen,
    And is highly pleasing to the eye.

These engines are the mechanic's pride
    And prove themselves equal to the strain,
As over the rails they smoothly glide
    Without in the least jarring the train.

Graceful and grand, they traverse the land,
    Like meteors through ambient space,
Applying the brakes and gritting sand,
    As over the road they swiftly race.

Splendid little engines that they are,
    Conceal'd like turtles under their shell,
They create no noise nor cause no jar,
    But perform their work wonderfully well.

I often think of these engines now,
    As something pertaining to the past,
 While thoughts of their being crown my brow,
    With peace and pleasure that could not last.

October, 1921

WILL YOU MISS ME WHEN I'M GONE?

Oh, friend, will you miss me when I'm gone,—
　　When this chair is vacant and forlorn,
And its empty space you gaze upon,
　　In the silent hours of night and morn?

Will you miss me in this room of pain
　　Where I have laid in misery's grasp,—
Where you have come again and again
　　My fevered hands to kindly clasp?

Will you miss me in the aisle and hall
　　Where often I walked to and fro,
When so frail, I feared I would fall,
　　And scarcely knew the right way to go?

Will you miss me in the dining room
　　Where the beautiful yellow bird sang,—
Where myrtle vines relieved the gloom
　　And juvenile joys with music rang?

Will you miss me from that bed of pain,
　　When I am feeble and far away,
As you look o'er the room where I've lain,
　　In memory of that painful day?

Will you miss me in anguish and pain
　　And wish for the help you render'd me
When under the strain of worried brain,
　　You will wait in vain for me to see?

Oh, friend, it is then you *will* miss me,
　　When reviewing events of the past,
And wonder why those things have to be
　　To over us such dark shadows cast.

Albuquerque, New Mexico, December 6 ,1921

WHEN THE FLOWERS BLOOM NEXT YEAR

When the garden flowers bloom next year,
　　Where, oh, where will we be, you and I?
Perhaps we'll be far away from here,
　　Or under the sod we may then lie.

When the fragrant flowers bloom next year,
　　Other men and women there may be,
To take the place of many, I fear,
　　Whose lot it will not be theirs to see.

When the golden flowers bloom next year,
　　And the fields are fresh with grass and grain,
There is a sweetness that will appear,
　　We long forever to see again.

When the dainty flowers bloom next year,
　　And the summer rains renew their stems,
It will to the gardens give new cheer,
　　For those who behold these floral gems.

When the fading flowers bloom next year,
　　In their declining stage of splendor,
When the autumn leaves are brown and sere—
　　Their beauty they will then surrender.

When the dying flowers bloom no more,
　　And the mournful winds of winter blow,
We, like others who have gone before,
　　Will, like them, slumber beneath the snow.

November, 1921

THE THREE THOUGHT-WORDS

The three thought-words that before me seem
    Like stars in the diadem of night,
Are fraught with feeling unto a dream
    That thrills my soul with ardent delight.

Beneath the depth of those three thought-words,
    There lies that sweetness *I* cannot tell,
Just as the flowers enchant the birds
    And hold them there in a magic spell.

'Tis not Fujiyama's snowy peak,
    *N*or that of beautiful Mt. Ranier,
That *I* am now inclined to speak,
    But something to me, by far, more dear.

Mountains cast their shadows in the skies,
    Rivers run on to the distant seas;
Flowers bloom in realms of paradise,
    While women bask on the beds of ease.

Men can climb the Andes' lofty range
    And command armies as Bonaparte,
But cannot explore mysteries, strange,
    *N*or fathom the depths of woman's heart.

From southern lands to the far northwest,
    Let my spirit wander where it will;
As that hazy hue instils my breast,
    So the three thought-words my bosom fill.

Oh, could we fathom the depths of thought,
 That is rarely, if ever, spoken,
It would reveal mental battles fought,
 Where hearts were hurt and often broken.

There remains within that dormant spark
 The embers of a latent pleasure,
If we can look through veneering dark
 And see the matrix's shining treasure.

Then 'tis the thought deeper than the word
 That we so quickly learn to revere,
As things unseen, we have often heard
 In our fond fancy, becomes more dear.

Oh! could we possess our souls to bless
 Those infinite joys on golden wings,
The philomel to the trees confess
 When in its branches he sweetly sings.

But the three thought-words before me stand
 Like former friends when they fondly meet,
Have within their meaning, something grand,
 Which literally is—"Ain't she sweet?"

UNDER THE MISTLETOE

If with me you will consent to go,
I'll meet you under the mistletoe;
Beneath the shade of cottonwood trees,
We'll bask in the balmy autumn breeze.

On the banks of the rippling river,
I'll thrust a dart to make you quiver,
And place upon your beautiful brow
A garland of leaves to show you how.

Sly Cupid comes in the fall of year,
To make his business very clear,
In the choice of an ardent desire,
While yet his dart is aflame with fire.

Then meet me under the mistletoe,
Where the sunlight falls and moon lights glow,
Where every day is a golden day
And every night a star-lit spray.

Oh, meet me under the mistletoe,
For that sacred pledge which you must know,
And unto you whom *I* much adore,
I'll promise my love forever more.

Victorville, California, November, 1921

FADING OF THE AUTUMN FLOWERS

Oh, must the little fragile flowers
    Surrender their beauty and their pride
To the relentless autumn powers
    After sweetly blooming side by side?

Through the summer days their strength was shown
    Against the dry and torrid weather;—
But those summer days have swiftly flown,
    And now they fade away forever.

Hyacinths and beautiful bluebells
    That gave the gardens such wondrous hues,
Ere the coming of autumn's cold spells,
    And ceasing of the fresh morning dews.

Mem'ries of them we fondly cherish,
    In the exquisite place they filled,
And lament that so soon they perish,
    When west winds their petals have chilled.

Leaves fast falling upon the bare ground,
    Drift hither and thither in the lanes,
As the wild winds of musical sound
    Blow through their branches in mournful strains.

A bird or a bee may stop to see,
    The change upon these fading flowers,
Then turn away and fly to a tree,
    To rest beneath its golden bowers.

A rabbit, perchance, will pass and pause,
　　To note the change that has taken place,
While man lingers long upon the cause
　　That affects also the human race.

Timid violets were first to go,
　　Followed by the sweet daffodils,
While the marigolds prepare for snow,
　　As their waving stems the cold wind chills.

Oh, lovely flowers, how fast they fade,
　　When once their festive season is gone;
They then look forth to the next decade,
　　As fall and winter pass swiftly on.

Sorrowful picture they now unfold,
　　And laws of nature, brought into it,
As the laws of man are thereby told,
　　With never a chance to eschew it.

It thus portrays the passing of one
　　Whose life, like flowers, faded away,
Long years ago, in her noonday sun,
　　When, alas!　she could no longer stay.

Then fading flowers that to the breeze
　　Their lowly heads are bent in despair,
So man his destiny clearly sees,
　　As he feels he too must enter there.

November, 1921

THE FIRST SNOWFALL

The corn is wither'd and crisp leaves blow
    O'er fields once green, but desolate now,
And all is chang'd with the falling snow,
    As through bare branches the wild winds plough.

How sudden and severe is the change,
    From green and gray and barren and brown,
We notice when the forest and range
    Is covered with this sheet of down.

The rabbits come out and look about,
    As if to survey the change in things,
And squirrels in the trees bark and shout,
    While the winter song bird lightly sings.

Sorrow to some is joy to others
    And snowbirds now come into their own,
While robins and wrens sought their covers
    In southern lands to which they have flown.

Mountain and plain all cover'd with snow,
    Assume a scene of the purest white,
While crystal rivers beneath them flow,
    Where the sun pours out her golden light.

Like old-time winters, the snow brings forth
    The graceful sleighs and merry sleigh bells,
As boys and girls in the frigid north,
    Surmise the secrets their sound foretells.

Then away they go o'er hill and dale,
  With flannels and furs wrapped round them,
Regardless of the cold, calm or gale
  And the irate parent's "Confound them."

The moon looking on in her brightness,
  Observes the speed in which they travel
And how their hearts are fraught with lightness,
  As their joyous reel they fast unravel.

Farther and farther they onward speed,
  Debating the while which way to go,
Where council of the preacher they need
  Will inform them what they want to know.

At last they reached this tranquil spot,
  Where beauty of night before them spread
Her grandeur for completing their plot,
  When the preacher his few words had said.

The irate parents, lonely and sad,
  Felt the effects of the first snowfall;
But John and Jane, now happy and glad,
  Thought it the grandest blessing of all.

Then homeward bound they turned their sleigh,
  All blithe and gay with its merry bells,
But wond'ring what the old folks would say,
  When they *found out* what the first snow spells.

November, 1921

THE AGED MAN'S SOLILOQUY

I feel the night of life coming on,
 As one by one old friends are falling,
And on my mind there begins to dawn
 Sad symptoms of that final calling.

The sunshine of life is fading fast;—
 Its music has no charms for me now,
And clouds of darkness, o'er me cast
 Their dismal shadows upon my brow.

Like flowers of spring that quickly pass
 With the withering wind's rapid rage,
Man lives but a brief spell, then, alas!
 Enters that dark and abysmal stage.

In life's varied journey o'er and o'er,
 I feel that *youth* is the era best
Of all this sojourn from shore to shore
 In which we are most freely blessed.

Children playing around the old homestead,
 Rekindle the flame of youth again,
Where often juvenile tears were shed,
 Then soothed as sunshine after rain.

Like leaves that fall and drift away,
 Man of his pride and power is shorn,
Leaving him the shadow of yesterday
 Depleted, dejected and forlorn!

Like faded flowers, with vigor gone,
    He feels the sting incident to age,
As younger people are coming on
    To take his place on life's active stage.

Oh! then where *is* the hope of the heart
    Against the gloom that around it falls,
When 'tis but a day 'til we depart
    Unto the mystery of His calls?

July, 1920

WHERE M*I*ND MEETS M*I*ND

In the quietude of Georgia Street
*I*t was our longing to often meet,
And spend the moments in tranquil talk
Instead of taking a toilsome walk.

If we were youthful and gay again,
These quiet moments would be in vain;
For then the heart is fond of pleasure
And knows not when it has its measure.

But when on Alice I sometimes call,
As the evening shades around me fall,
I think our lives, like the day, is gone
And night upon us begins to dawn.

There comes a time within our being,
When from worry we feel like fleeing,
And grasp the chance to converse awhile
With those who lend a consoling smile.

It thus transpires when friendship is keen,
The happiest hours are often seen
While we're enrapt'd in this pleasant way,
As nightfall follows the close of day.

Then across the street where palm trees grow,
Young people are passing to and fro;
Recalling to us that happy stage
That precedes the coming of old age.

How true it is that our desires change
As we enter on the downward range,
And the youthful charms that lit my brow
Are, alas! to me as nothing now.

Faithful friendship in its gracious way,
Prolongs our blessings from day to day,
And blessed are the garlands of love
When to us they come from Him above.

So onward we strive from year to year,
Omitting things that in youth were dear,
Until at last, from the closing door,
I'll disappear to return no more.

TREE OF THE TROSSACHS

There is a birch tree in Trossachs Glen
    Whose beauty of bark and foliage
Fascinates alike, women and men,
    As they behold its beautiful stage.

Beneath the pleasant, refreshing shade,
    There flows a sweet little mountain stream,
Caressing the shores of glen and glade
    With the magic of a summer dream.

Its leaves are soft and smooth and mellow,
    As through them the sunlight finds its way,
With blending of the brown and yellow,
    In the haze of a beautiful day.

Along the banks of this crystal stream,
    Green bushes and vines are entwined
Into the realms of another dream,
    With all the beauty nature can find.

There is not a more enchanting sight,
    In the Trossach's wonderful array,
Of that which is viable and bright,
    In the charm of a sweet summer day.

Through hazy heights to the mountain's peak
    There stretches one grand, seductive view,
Where birds and bees in their pleasure seek
    The sweetness of the refreshing dew.

Oh, the charms of these Scottish bluebells,
    And the pink heather that underlies
The soft shade of the exquisite dells
    That reflect their colors in the skies.

Tree of the Trossachs, supremely sweet,
    With fragrant flowers beneath thy shade,
Where heaven and earth serenely meet,
    And stamp their presence on hill and glade.

Oh, tree of the Trossachs, I behold,
    In this beautiful, beautiful glen,
Thy bark of silver and leaves of gold,
    That charm the soul of women and men.

Loch Lomond, Scotland, July, 1921

THE COMPLETENESS OF CREATION

The exquisite flowers clothe the fields,
  The richest roses perfume the air,
The nightly dewdrops their sweetness yields
  To the morning sunbeam's golden glare.

The mountains have their majestic heights,
  The scalloped hills their graceful mould,
The virgin forests, their lurid nights,
  And the rolling plains their tinge of gold.

The sea-gulls rest on the ocean's crest,
  The squirrels in the tallest of trees,
The robin in its fortified nest,
  And the inland thrush far from the seas.

But the desert, beneath scorching skies,
  Precludes the charms of animal traits,—
Neither bird nor bee above it flies,
  As approaching heat of day it waits.

Over the summit of yonder peak,
  The stars display their wondrous array,
As they light the hills, barren and bleak,
  After the close of a summer day.

In twilight silence, the landscape now
  Stretches away to the star-lit skies,
Where, in enchantment, we know not how,
  Their tranquil being supremely vies.

Profoundly quiet, the evening hours
    Pervade the desert, now gray and dull
From lack of rain and lack of flowers,
    Yet withal, sublime and beautiful.

Even grander than the grandest day,
    Night is to me, as I see it here,
Where myriads of stars o'er me play;
    Strongest proof of God's eternal sphere.

There is nothing to pollute the peace
    That here exists between earth and skies,—
Like the ancient Marathon of Greece,
    It retains its splendid memories.

Thus we see in nature's perfect plans,
    From distant desert to the mountains,
There is an invisible eye that scans
    The earth and air and flowing fountains.

All nature has her appointments plann'd
    In the working of the universe,
And will, in due time, reveal her hand
    For what is wiser or what is worse.

Then man alone is left to ponder
    Upon the marvelous works of God,
As he beholds with awe and wonder
    Mystic realms through which he seeks to trod.

November, 1920

NIGHT AT THE NEEDLES

(The Needles proper are on the left bank of the Colorado River in Arizona, twenty-five miles southeast of the town of Needles, California, and from the beautiful cantilever bridge afford one of the most impressive and fascinating nocturnal vistas in all this desiccated country.)

Night has enchantments across the seas,
    From Scotland's ever beautiful lands,
And the pretty Spanish Pyrenees
    To Arabia's distant drifting sands.

But night at The Needles is supreme
    In a specific class of its own,
Where primitive earth lies in a dream,
    And nothing but stillness there is known.

The clear blue skies and silvery moon
    Light up this enchanting desert view,
In all the glory of midnight June,
    As falls the light in a hazy hue.

India boasts of her great Khyber Pass,
    Her River Jumna and Taj Mahah;
Her lofty mountains and waving grass
    And Tiger Hill, that excites with awe.

Egypt has her noted River Nile,
    Lybian desert and moonlit skies;
Her beautiful sunsets all the while
    And afterglow that over them rise.

But The Needles, stern, straight, stolid Needles,
    In their silent, majestic rearing,
Have not the song of summer beetles
    To make a sound within their hearing.

Their rugged points penetrate the skies
    In the ultra-quietude of night,
While the majesty of heaven lies
    In disbursing her most marv'lous light.

Sharp crags that point, like wild boars' bristles
    To the beautiful, brilliant stars;
While the stream runs through desert thistles,
    T'ward the ocean's ever open bars.

Serenely stand these eternal peaks
    In an isolated world of their own;
Where the clear canopy never leaks,
    And the nightly stars have always shown.

Oh! grandeur of The Needles at night,
    Where heaven and earth try to excel,
When the light of moon and stars unite
    In their infinite, glorious spell.

Then let us console our spirit here,
    Where not even the song of beetles
Breaks the silence of the atmosphere,
    In this charming "Night at The Needles."

November, 1921

DIAMONDS OF THE DESERT

Diamonds of the desert daze the eyes
Under Arizona's bright blue skies;
When the morning sunbeams on them rest,
Their brilliance is seen at their best.

Grass and bushes with brightness beaming,
While in their beauty they are teeming,
With multiplied thousands of these gems,
That cluster around their leaves and stems.

In fullness of the morning sunlight,
Their iridescence portrays a sight,
Richer by far than Queen Mary's crown,
While in the zenith of her renown.

Myriads of these bright little gems
Cover the desert with diadems
Of the most beautiful, real designs
That the connoisseur in nature finds.

These sparkling "diamonds of the desert"
Outshine the jewels of Mrs. Mesert,
That in our dreams are so beguiling,
And keep us in a mood for smiling.

But be prepar'd for deceptions' ruse
That leads you on an alluring cruise
Through silv'ry waters and golden skies,
Before the phantom takes wings and flies.

These wonderful gems in their glory
To which *I* must ascribe this story,
And admit to you at any cost
They're no more nor less than crystal *frost*.

December, 1921

_____

TWO EXTREMES

There's a little girl whose face is fair,
    Whose form is lithe and very slender;
Her eyes ultra-bright and black her hair
    While yet her hands are soft and tender.

She's very sweet and often present
    And I like to meet her when I can,
For she's so cheerful and so pleasant,
    And her name is Atlee Haldeman.

There is a man in this same hotel
    Whose form is bent and step very slow;
His eyes are dim and his feet foretell
    That age upon him begins to show.

He's good as gold, though a little old,
    And I like to meet him ev'ry day;
For as the story has oft been told,
    He's eighty-four, and not long to stay.

Thus here I behold the two extremes
    Of sweet little girl and grand old man
That often appear to us in dreams,
    As only such realities can.

IS THERE ANYTHING BEYOND THE BRAIN?

Is there anything beyond the brain,
    Within this human machine of ours,
That from this time to the days of *C*ain,
    Has enrapt our profoundest powers?

As the light radiates from the sun,
    And energy is convey'd through wire,
So is life from the time it begun,
    Measured by the things we acquire.

As the boiler furnishes the steam,
    Through immaculate system of flues,
The brain is the source through which we gleam,
    All energy that our bodies use.

Each sensitive nerve of our being,
    Radiates from the base of the brain;—
The optic, through the eye, in seeing,
    Performs its part like clouds during rain.

This intricate system has a base
    From which all knowledge is supplied,
And 'tis that base in the human race
    That gave to all who've lived and died.

*N*erves and arteries are sparks of life
    Which are govern'd by sense of the brain,
As in orchestra, sound of the fife
    Supplies a deep, harmonious strain.

The seat and sense of joy and sorrow,
    Our ev'ry nerve reports to the brain;
From tips of toes and spinal marrow,
    They form one endless, sensitive chain.

Mind and muscle have their center there,
    And if we presume there is a soul,
We're inclin'd to think it will be fair
    To place in within the brain's control.

Then as clouds are essential to rain,
    And do their part in its descending,
So are the functions of the brain
    Supreme in all the themes contending.

Is there anything beyond the brain,—
    Mental, physical or otherwise,—
We can, by the utmost effort gain
    Knowledge of what the future implies?

There's nothing brighter than the sun's light,
    That we behold in the sublime skies,
Nor nothing darker than depths of night,
    As its intensity multiplies.

Thus it is seen the truth of these things,
    And the ultimate proof that we gain,
By evidence their existence brings,
    That there *is* nothing beyond the brain.

Sheep follow the leaders of their flocks,
    Regardless of the way they're going,
And the sea birds seek refuge on rocks,
    When wild waves around them are flowing.

As the crowning sheaf upon the shock,
  I repeat the question once again;
Is there any refuge on the rock
  That exists beyond the human brain?

Oh! my God, *I* must humbly confess
  That all *I* can learn from earthly source,
Leads me but into the wilderness
  From which there is but little recourse.

Tell me then if there *is* anything
  Beyond the profound depths of the brain,
That to my mind will more clearly bring
  Bright sunshine, after the gloom of rain?

January, 1922

TO ROSALIA

Through intricate films of the distance
　　There brightly shines a beautiful star;
In the sweetness of her irresistance
　　I often wonder how far, how far.

Oh! could I fly in aerial plane
　　O'er mountains and meadows to her side,
I fancy the joy that I should gain,
　　Within my soul would forever abide.

As blow the winds over land and sea
　　And caress the shores of far-off isles,
So does her image appear to me
　　In the sweetness of her sunny smiles.

As the sun lights up the mountain's crest
　　Beyond the faraway hazy skies,
So does her mem'ry within my breast
　　Recall the light of her sparkling eyes.

If I should lose this beautiful gem
　　And naught but mem'ry of her remain,
The brilliance of the diadem
　　Would never return to me again.

Oh! tell me then, will her love decay
　　Throughout the passing of future years,
And leave me in a state of dismay
　　That fills the heart with trouble and tears?

MEMORIES OF MALTRATA

Dedicated to Mrs. E. Y. Cuthbert, who is familiar with the transcendent beauty of
this charming place.)

Memories of Maltrata, Mexico,
    Beset my mind with renew'd vision,
As after sunset, the golden glow
    Remains to prolong our decision.

Oh, beautiful Maltrata, that lies
    Like a pearl in its translucent shell,
Beneath the ever tropical skies,
    And the charms of their wonderful spell.

Oh, beautiful valley, lying low
    Under grasses of velvety green,—
Nourished by the soft, melting snow,
    From Orizaba, in the distance seen.

Tropical trees and flowers galore
    Beautify this land of paradise,
While birds in their boughs, forever more,
    Bear melodies that over them rise.

Nestled below the mountain's crest,
    This little town in her native pride,
Clings close as the noble eagle's nest,
    Unto its beautiful sloping side.

Trains in their serpentine course, descend
    This picturesque stretch of Alpine land,
Where earth and heaven serenely blend,
    In combination supremely grand.

Then entering at the eastern door,
    Into the bewilderments of this spot,
Our senses are charmed more and more,
    As we behold nature's grandest plot.

The landscape that expands far away,
    Over vale and valley to the east,
Here presents a beautiful array
    Of golden colors on which to feast.

Oh, Maltrata, fairest in the world,
    'Neath the shade of Orizaba's crest,
Thy vista stands like skylights hurled
    Over the apex of nature's breast.

A filmy cloud hanging in the sky,
    Casts its frail shadow upon the town,
Where fragrance of flowers underlie
    Lisping zephyrs, as the sun goes down.

If there is a more beautiful sight
    In the *C*reator's grandest display,
Than this vast valley and the mountain's height,
    Where, oh, where in this world does it lay?

Then may thy memories linger long,
    Upon the minds of those who have seen
Thy beauty, and heard thy peaceful song,
    Through the fleeting years that intervene.

December, 1921

LET ME SLEEP BY THE SOUND OF THE SEA

(Memories of the east coast of Guatemala.)
(Dedicated to my esteemed friend, Dr. Hal Foster, Kansas City, U.S.A.)

Wave follows wave from the ocean's crest
    And exhaust their force against the land,
Then recede again upon the breast
    Of the rolling tide, supremely grand.

From the frigid to the torrid zone,
    The lapping waters caress the shores
Of every island that is known,
    From *China* to the southern Azores.

From the denuded pines of Skagway
    To old *India*'s spreading banyan tree,
Murmuring waters beside them play,
    As they cast their shade upon the sea.

Then to sleep by the sound of the sea,
    With my soul sooth'd by the water's voice,
Through the length of all eternity,
    Is my fanciful and final choice.

Where palm trees grow and the myrtle vines,
    In those far-away tropical isles,
I often think, as my mind inclines,
    Of the balmy breeze and ocean's smiles.

As sunlight cheers wherever it shines,
    So the waters soothe our troubled hearts,
And golden riches are in the mines,
    If we but see what nature imparts.

It remains withal a foregone fact
  That whatever conditions may be,
If the desire is back of the act,
  Sleep is sweet by the sound of the sea.

After the storm, there follows a calm
  Which we behold in nature divine,
That quiets our soul with gracious balm
  When the sun again begins to shine.

When day has surrendered to night,
  Sparkling stars appear without number,
And the moon in her tropical light,
  Serenely shines on those who slumber.

Subdued the waves, then back they roll,
  To mingle again as one who's lost,
In realms of power, beyond control,
  As to and fro they're roughly tossed.

Sublime the waters portray their part
  In nature's supreme and perfect plans
That thrill the chords of the human heart,
  As unto us her glory expands.

Then turbulent tides that never cease
  Impart a consoling charm to me,—
And to prolong their incumbent peace,
  Let me sleep by the sound of the sea.

THE POWER OF A FLOWER

Oh! thou delicate little flower,
    Blooming on hilltops and mountain side;
Dost thou know the infinite power
    That lies within thy reticent pride?

When storms have swept the forest and plain
    And left them in a state of despair,
Your fragrance and beauty still remain
    Under the guidance of Divine care.

When we lie low in the throes of pain,
    And long for the help of God's wise will,
You cheer our mind and console our brain
    With a solace that our bosoms fill.

Thy presence calms the anger of men,
    And soothes the soul of the distressed,
While wreathing for them a diadem,
    That they have not before possessed.

There lies within thy exquisite mold,
    The symbol of purity and love,
With influence like the charms of gold,
    Yet modest as the most docile dove.

You bridge the span of many a plan,
    Along the pathway of friendship's course,
And assist the woman to win the man,
    With your refined and floral force.

Wealth and poverty you bless the same,
    By your presence, wherever growing,—
Whether in wild woods or gardens tame,—
    As you perfume the breezes blowing.

Oh! mighty power of a flower,
    Over the juvenile and old age,
As strength thou dost bestow ev'ry hour,
    Through the term of thy beautiful stage.

Your timid aspects sometimes foretell
    The secret sentiments of our hearts,
And hold us in an enchanted spell,
    While Cupid sharpens his arrow darts.

Then let me dwell *on* that happy spell
    In faraway London's busy Strand,
Of the pleasure that to her befell,
    When flowers were plac'd at her command.

January, 1922

THE GOLDEN DAYS OF OLDEN DAYS

Oh! the golden days of olden days,
    Will they ne'er return to me again?
Since *I*'ve grown old and changed my ways
    Their joys and pleasures no more remain.

Could we unite the present and past,
    And make one grand and glorious *Now*,
How sweet would be that model to cast,
    *I*f only someone would show us *how!*

We barely feel the fervor and glow
    Of the butterfly's beautiful wings,
Until he's gone in the fleeting show,
    That his bright presence upon us brings.

Then when we review the long spent past,
    And wish again for pleasures in vain,
Find that sunshine does not always last,
    But often follow'd by dismal rain.

We see no more the butterfly's gold—
    His roseate sides and gilded crest;
His story to us is hereby told
    In plainest language that fits us best.

Thus the golden days of olden days,
    Come not to us in succeeding years;
For we have changed our former ways,
    While they remain the same, it appears.

February, 1922

DAWN TO DARKNESS

(*Dedicated to my only brother, Willard E. Decker*)

As dawn of day breaks over the walls
    And spreads its light on the rolling fields,
The balm of morning our soul enthralls
    With a golden gleam that o'er us steals.

So is the boy, all buoyant and bright,
    Entering upon his life-long course,
Ready to play and ready to fight
    As he expands in juvenile force.

But intrepid youth, if you could know
    The stormy regions that lie before,
You might, perchance, hesitate to go
    Across the chasms you'll have to explore.

The sun advancing, chases the moon
    Away in the Hesperian skies,
As with the approaching hours of noon
    Effulgence of light around them lies.

Song birds and bees harbor in the trees,
    And display their delight in living,
While man is monarch of all he sees,
    And feels the joy of nature's giving.

All is roseate around noonday,
    And sunshine supreme in its control,
As before it, clouds vanish away,
    Leaving scenes that emulate the soul.

The universe at its ultra-height,
    Like man, makes a supernal display;
Then for a time, grants a respite
    To glories that change and fade away.

When we reach the zenith of this life,
    Then dwell a spell on its changing stage,
We feel the bitterness of the knife
    That keenly cuts us in our old age.

As the ancient Greek general laugh'd
    In viewing his army, ten thousand strong,
But was observed to be chafed
    When to his mind, something seemed wrong.

Then when his joy had turned to tears
    And he was asked why his weeping,
He replied,—"Within a hundred years
    These splendid men will all be sleeping."

The great Greek general with his men
    Have long since passed into their tombs;
So with the present, as was it then,
    The brightest lights have their coming dooms.

Like the Greek army, men rise and fall
    Between the dawn of day and its close,
And surrender to the final call
    That comes to them in defeating blows.

Sad is the sight that we look upon
    When the noonday of life is passed—
When flowers of our pathway are gone
    And shadows o'er us begin to cast.

We realize the shortness of time
    That is to us allotted on earth,
Compared with the eternal chime
    Of bells before and after our birth.

We see the shades of night drawing nigh,
    As the evening sun is sinking low,
And feel the pain of a pensive sigh
    As o'er us darkness begins to grow.

February, 1922

FIELDS AND FOREST

Oh, beautiful fields and forest green,
  Laden with the austral wind's perfume;
How sweet the sight that is to be seen
  When youthful memories you resume.

Dogwood blossoms in pure white and gold
  Enhance the forest in their own way,
As structures of beauty they unfold
  *I*n the most beautiful month of May.

Pink sweet Williams and bleeding hearts
  With the violet Johnny-jump-ups,
Add a thrill of rapture with their darts
  To the charm of blooming buttercups.

The air is sweet with scent of flowers,
  The trees impart their fresh foliage,
The soft sunlight peers through the bowers
  And lightens up the enchanted stage.

Oh, the exquisite charm of this day
  In fields and forest and skies above—
A perfect day in the month of May
  To fill our hearts with infinite love!

Beautiful flowers that clothe the fields
  In delicate tints of red and blue,
And amber skies, as the sunset yields
  Its rapt'rous colors of brightest hue.

Oh, the grandeur and glory of it all,
　　As these flowers with each other vie;
Unto my soul they profoundly call
　　Attention to what within them lie.

Thus we see in this simple story,
　　King Solomon, in all his array,
Was not so clothed in his glory
　　As the fragrant flowers here display.

THE SETTING SUN

The crimson sun is now sinking low
　　Beyond the high Hesperian skies,
Lining them with a glorious glow
　　As the day most beautifully dies.

Great tiers of those gorgeous, golden shreds
　　Of suspended clouds, aflame with fire,
Across the heavens their beauty spreads,
　　Then vanish in space, higher and higher.

Oh! that this grandeur fade not away
　　*I*nto the solemnity of night,
But in beauty and brilliance stay,
　　To prolong this magnificent sight.

But the sun's grand day's duty is done
　　And its bright colors vanishing fast,
Proving that even what *it* begun,
　　Is endow'd with charms that cannot last.

MEDITATION

When the sun sinks low *I* think of thee
As a shining pearl beneath the sea,
Washed brighter by the onward roll
Of the constant waves that charm my soul.

Oh could I stay this longing for thee
And let my spirit once more be free,
I'd seek the joy of some far off shore
And there remain forever more.

I'd watch the waves in their restless plight
For tidings of thee both day and night
And when the sun give way to the moon,
I'd flatter myself you're coming soon.

Then under the light of star-lit skies
We'd taste the pleasure of paradise,
As moonbeams played upon the sea
I would fondly think and think of thee.

A foamy surf that lashes the shore
Enchants the sea gulls that o'er it soar
And leaves a trace of nautical tones
As receding waves utter their moans.

Oh, the grandeur of the deep blue sea,
How its majesty appeals to me
And fills my heart with ardent desire
To join its strains of vibrant choir!

The mermaid there is free from care
When the nights are calm and days are fair,
Sublime the sight of nautical night '
Where the stars look on then take their flight.

Endless, boundless, tractless depths divine,
Bright and glorious the sun doth shine
Upon the glistening ocean's breast
As if its grandeur it was to test.

But where is she, the pearl of my heart,
Whose absence keenly quickens the smart
And leaves me in the straits of despair
That weight my soul with sorrow and care?

Her image has been taken away,—
It was too sweet for this mortal clay,—
And now in vain, I search land and sea
For pleasures that come no more to me.

THE END OF THE TRAIL

In writing these final lines, *I* feel
    As one, who after a long sojourn,
Reverts to the scenes that o'er him steal,
    When in his heart past incidents burn.

We realize that our time is brief,
    And soon fond friends will know us no more;
For death lurks like an insipid thief
    Along life's highway, from shore to shore.

Our journey in the wilderness lies
    And is fraught with many clouds and gales,
While to the future our spirit cries
    For something better beyond its vales.

I saw a poor girl from Montreal,
    Whose face was pale and her form was frail;
She tried to combat the final call
    That mark'd her for the end of the trail.

Her dismal days were fading away,
    Her patient mind was weary and worn,
Yet there seemed to around her play
    The radiance of a brighter morn.

Thus it is; we're passing, passing fast,
    Toward that solemn and awful change;
Our lot, like others, we know is cast
    And we will soon "cross over the range."

Oh, my friends, what an alarming thought
    This transition from mortal life brings,
As in the midst of it, we are caught
    And borne away like lambs on eagles' wings.

There's no appeal from this sad ordeal
    That lies at the end of our life line;
Yet in a way, we are taught to feel
    There's hope and help in the great Divine.

To those whose feet are weary and worn
    From constant burdens of worldly weight,—
To those whose hearts are sad and forlorn,
    There's relief in this eternal state.

As we review the long lane of life,
    With its pleasures and pain, as they came;
We find the sting of struggle and strife
    To one and all, pretty much the same.

Oh! for the world if we could live on
    And continue in one joyous spell;—
But like others who have come and gone,
    We must prepare for final farewell.

Then as I close these last lines, dear friends,
    From what we might term life's falling veil,
It is to you that my love extends,
    As I approach "The End of the Trail."